VICTOR RIPP

HELL'S TRACES

Victor Ripp is the author of *Moscow to Main Street*, *Pizza in Pushkin Square*, and *Turgenev's Russia*. His fiction has appeared in the *Ontario Review* and *The Antioch Review*. He has taught at Cornell University and the University of Virginia. He lives in New Jersey.

ALSO BY VICTOR RIPP

Pizza in Pushkin Square: What Russians Think About Americans and the American Way of Life

Moscow to Main Street: Among the Russian Emigrés

Turgenev's Russia: From "Notes of a Hunter" to "Fathers and Sons"

HELL'S TRACES

HELL'S TRACES

**ONE MURDER, TWO FAMILIES,
THIRTY-FIVE HOLOCAUST
MEMORIALS**

VICTOR RIPP

FARRAR, STRAUS AND GIROUX   NEW YORK

Farrar, Straus and Giroux
175 Varick Street, New York 10014

The Library of Congress has cataloged the hardcover edition as follows:
Names: Ripp, Victor, author.
Title: Hell's traces : one murder, two families, thirty-five Holocaust memorials /
    Victor Ripp.
Description: First edition. | New York : Farrar, Straus and Giroux, 2017. |
    Includes bibliographical references.
Identifiers: LCCN 2016033254 | ISBN 9780865478336 (hardback) |
    ISBN 9780374713638 (e-book)
Subjects: LCSH: Holocaust memorials—Europe. | Holocaust memorials. |
    Holocaust, Jewish (1939–1945)—France—Biography. | Holocaust, Jewish
    (1939–1945)—Germany—Biography. | Ripp family. | Ripp, Victor—Travel. |
    BISAC: HISTORY / Holocaust. | HISTORY / Jewish.
Classification: LCC D804.17 .R57 2017 | DDC 940.53/1864094—dc23
LC record available at https://lccn.loc.gov/2016033254

Paperback ISBN: 978-0-374-53748-7

Designed by Abby Kagan

www.fsgbooks.com
www.twitter.com/fsgbooks • www.facebook.com/fsgbooks

P1

In memory of my parents,
Solomon and Gita Ripp

KAHAN FAMILY*

Chaim, great-grandfather of author

Malka, great-grandmother of author

Aron, son of Chaim and Malka

David, son of Chaim and Malka

Marie, daughter of Chaim and Malka

Bendet, son of Chaim and Malka

Baruch-Tanchum, son of Chaim and Malka

Pinchas, son of Chaim and Malka

Zina (née Golodetz), wife of Pinchas

Lolia (Leonid), son of Pinchas and Zina

Tani (Tanchum) Cohen-Mintz, grandson of Baruch-Tanchum

RIPP FAMILY*

Lev (Leima), grandfather of author

Eva, grandmother of author

Sula Cholenay (née Ripp), daughter of Lev and Eva

Roger Cholenay, husband of Sula

Aronchik (Aron), son of Lev and Eva

Vera (née Liebermann), wife of Aronchik

Olga Liebermann, mother of Vera

Alexandre, son of Aronchik and Vera

Monia (Solomon), son of Lev and Eva, husband of Gita

Gita (née Kahan), daughter of Pinchas and Zina, wife of Monia

Paul, son of Monia and Gita

Victor, son of Monia and Gita

*Only those family members mentioned in the text

Baltic
Sea

LATVIA

LITHUANIA

RUSSIA

RUSSIA

Dnieper R.

Minsk ★

Grodno •   Neman R.   Bobruisk
                        •Shchedrin
            •Nesvizh

BELARUS

Vistula R.

Warsaw ★

POLAND

UKRAINE

Kraków •
•Auschwitz

SLOVAKIA

MOLDOVA

★Budapest   ROMANIA

HUNGARY

                    0 Miles   100   Black
                                                    Sea
                    0 Kilometers   100

                                    Danube R.

CROATIA

© 2017 Jeffrey L. Ward

HELL'S TRACES

ALEXANDRE RIPP WAS MY COUSIN on my father's side. In July 1942, the French police in Paris, acting for the German military government, arrested him—though "arrested" suggests more force than needed to take a three-year-old child into custody. Alexandre was killed in Auschwitz two months later.

Over the years, I spoke about my cousin very rarely. I could see that the story of his ordeal was of interest to most people only when patched onto the story of the Holocaust, and that had been told many times over. So many books, films, photographs—there seemed no space left for Alexandre. Then something happened that showed me I was wrong.

I was in Berlin's Jewish Museum to see the exhibit *Berlin Transit*, about the influx of Russian Jews into Berlin in the 1920s. The Kahans, my family on my mother's side, had been a wealthy and philanthropically active émigré family in that city, which made them a good exemplar of the exhibit's theme. Two rooms were devoted to the Kahans.

After an hour spent considering the mementos and documents and photos and wondering how all of it might be connected to the life I was living (ex-professor of Russian literature, comfortable Colonial with paid-up mortgage, three-year-old Honda in the driveway), I decided to have a look at the rest of the museum. The layout was unusual. The architect had designed a building that was itself a sort of exhibit. Strolling through it should be as meaningful an experience as looking at any of the paintings hanging on the walls.

The scheme of the interior kept me moving along toward an intersection of three corridors, two of which especially got my attention. One was marked "Axis of Exile" and opened onto a garden. The other, "Axis of the Holocaust," ended in an askew, dimly lit room that suggested a prison cell or, once I let my imagination go, a physical analog of shapeless horror. That Jews had few options as the Nazis took control was old news, but the Kahan family exhibit that I had just seen made me look at those two corridors in a particularly personal way.

The Kahan family in Berlin, several generations' worth, numbered some thirty people, and without exception they escaped the Final Solution. When Hitler came to power, most moved to Palestine; others went westward, eventually to the United States. They had found their way through the first corridor, but my cousin Alexandre had been forced into the second. His mother, both grandmothers, three granduncles, a grandaunt, and three of his cousins also died in the Holocaust. And while the Kahans got a commemorative exhibit, the Ripps who were killed by the Nazis didn't even have a grave.

Of course the museum had its own goals, and that was fine. Museums have to attract an audience, and they design their exhibits accordingly. My sense of a miscarriage was personal. In my mind, the Ripps and the Kahans were linked. My father married into the Kahan family, but that did not make him any less Alexandre's uncle. My mother was Alexandre's aunt, but she never stopped thinking of herself as Zina Kahan's daughter. But a kinship diagram wouldn't tell the whole story. The two families were socially and emotionally intertwined.

If the histories of the two families were plotted on a graph, there would be numerous points of convergence. One would mark the German occupation of Paris, when Alexandre's father, Aron—always Aronchik to friends and family—hid in the Kahans' vacated business office on Rue de la Bienfaisance. That convergence deserves an asterisk to connote a wrinkle of fate. The office was vacant only because the Kahans had managed to get out of Paris just before the Nazis took control.

There were also moments when the lines on the graph would be far apart, as the two families followed their dissimilar paths. The Ripps went from Grodno, in what is now Belarus, to Paris, while the Kahans began in Poland before passing through Baku, in Azerbaijan, and pausing for a decade in Berlin. But the lines would still be on the same graph because they equally traced how the two families were pushed across the map of Europe by the twentieth century's catastrophes.

One more link between the families: Put photos of me and Alexandre both at age three side by side. Everyone remarks on the resemblance. But there's a difference that shadows the resemblance. I escaped the Nazi trap and Alexandre didn't. His murder is a key moment in the history of the two families, casting a bleak light on many events that went before.

When I got back to the States after seeing the Berlin exhibit, I tried to write about the two families. But I couldn't get it to work. The words lay lifelessly on the page as in some antique chronicle. The events occurred long ago, I couldn't grasp what made them move one way and not another. I had to find something in the world around me that would make the past appear more vivid.

That, I realized when I thought about it, is what memorials do. They exist in the present but take their meanings from the past, they bring history closer, and that was what I needed. I understood that memorials typically evoke the lives of famous men and women and events of global significance, not the histories of two families like the Ripps and the Kahans who had little claim to public attention. But that was only one way to look at it.

Consider this: When I saw Maya Lin's Vietnam Veterans Memorial, my first thoughts were about how political decisions made thousands of miles from the battlefield had caused many Americans to die. I recalled that politicians talked of communism on the march, about something called the Domino Theory. The memorial prompted thoughts about the sweep of great historical events. That was my initial response, but it was not the only one. I thought about my own connection to the Vietnam War—how luck and circumstance had kept me out of harm's way, how one friend escaped the draft by going to Canada, how another was a medic in the Mekong Delta. Memorials can trigger different messages, some more personal than others.

The story of the Kahans and the Ripps that I wanted to tell was ultimately a Holocaust story, so it would be Holocaust memorials that I should see. I planned to visit as many as I could include in a short itinerary. They would certainly remind me of how the Nazis killed six million Jews, and a refresher of that history lesson is always worthwhile. But I hoped that some memorials would also spark to life the story about the different destinies of the Kahans and the Ripps.

I decided to go and see the Holocaust memorial in New Jersey's Liberty State Park. It was a random choice, but I had to begin somewhere and it wasn't that far from home. Negotiating the exuberant traffic on the turnpike was probably not the best way to get into the right mood, but once off the exit ramp and into the park I slipped into another mode of existence. The tree-lined driveway was some two miles long, and by the time I reached its end I felt something approaching reverence. New Jersey doesn't often get this still and quiet. It helped that it was the middle of a workweek—only one family of picnickers to be seen, a few cyclists, a virtually empty parking lot.

The memorial is set off by itself in a treeless space that opens onto a view of the Hudson and the Manhattan skyline beyond. It is some fifteen feet high and consists of two blackened bronze figures. A helmeted American soldier, pants tucked into his boots, carries a concentration camp survivor in his arms. The soldier is robust and strong—he needs only one hand to hold up his burden. The other figure is so thin that his ribs are visible, and his limp body suggests a nearness to death. He clings to the soldier to keep from falling.

The inscription on the pedestal, "Dedicated to America's Role of Preserving Freedom and Rescuing the Oppressed," underscores the obvious. The soldier is the focal point of the memorial, the concentration camp survivor is a prop to emphasize the soldier's generosity of spirit, his heroic nature. And the Holocaust was an opportunity for Pax Americana to show its stuff.

When I looked beyond the memorial, Ellis Island and the Statue of Liberty loomed in the middle distance. The triptych—memorial, island, statue—was almost certainly not accidental. Grouped with those two national icons, the memorial took on some of their significance. It became part of a celebration of the values America endorses. "The Star-Spangled Banner" playing in the background was all that was needed to complete the composition.

Heading back to my car, I stopped off at the information desk to pick up some literature. I learned that the memorial was created by Nathan Rapoport, a Polish sculptor whose works are also on exhibit in Warsaw and Jerusalem. That was information worth noting. It underscored something that should have been obvious but kept slipping out of focus—that the memorial I had just seen was not the spirit of the Jewish people set in stone with no human intervention, but something built by one man with his own ideas about the Holocaust. It was a Nathan Rapoport production.

I had been struck by how few people were in the park. When I asked the ranger on duty about this, he spoke up for his domain.

"You should see it here on a holiday. Fourth of July, when the big ships sail by into the harbor, this place jumps."

I could picture it. Fathers and sons playing catch, barbecues heating up, teenagers reveling. America at play, at its unbuttoned best. But what did it do to the meaning of the memorial to be in the middle of such pleasures and excitements? The aesthetic merit of this memorial aside—agitprop, in my opinion, grandiose—the trip had taught me something important about all memorials. The setting counts. A nation's spirit always seeps into the meaning of a memorial placed within its borders. Liberty Park is likely an extreme example, but any Holocaust memorial set in America would have some Americana in its system. Which is why I had to go to Europe. That was where the destinies of the Ripps and the Kahans had played out.

There were many memorials to choose from. My web search brought up a map showing close to a thousand. The icons were clustered in Central Europe, where guilt was thick on the ground, and that was where I would start my trip. I packed a laptop and a camera, checked that my passport was valid, and got going.

Could a stone pillar or a bronze plaque or whatever else constitutes a memorial cause events that took place more than seven decades ago to appear vivid? I would soon find out.

My first stop was Germany, where a recent survey found more than two hundred Holocaust memorials. This suggests how strenuously Germans have been trying to come to terms with their past. But it also suggests how hard it is to get that business right.

Berlin's Memorial to the Murdered Jews of Europe is the most visited Holocaust memorial in the country, included in just about every tourist itinerary, and that was where I would go first. But I wanted to get some local comment before having a look. Michael Cullen was the editor of *Jewish Voices from Germany*, an English-language monthly, and a mutual friend had told me he had been active in the debates surrounding the memorial's construction. When we met at a café near his apartment in the Charlottenburg district, it didn't take much to get Cullen talking.

"It took fifteen years to get an agreement to move forward. Why? No blueprint to follow. A country honoring those it killed. Not the usual thing, is it?

"Then the location. Some wanted it in the camps, the scene of the crime. Many Jews insisted on the city center, so Berliners would have to face their past every day. Everyone had an opinion. One camp survivor insisted it shouldn't be where he would pass it on the way to work each morning.

"A big problem was the design. One proposal was a field of yellow flowers in the shape of a Star of David like what the Nazis forced Jews to wear on their clothing. The Jews as victims. Several proposals were like that. There was a lot of shouting against that approach. As I said, everyone had an opinion."

Cullen had the world-weary manner of a veteran who had made it back from the trenches. He had fought the good fight and had his war stories as testimony to his efforts, but the battle was behind him.

I asked him if he was okay with the memorial as it was finally designed.

"Let's say I've come to terms with it. It's good that it's so abstract that it can have different meanings for different people. The Holocaust was a lot of things, not just one thing."

A soft rain was falling when I arrived at the memorial, which accentuated its bleak unwelcoming aspect. There was no marked entrance and no obvious path through the 2,711 granite steles that were arranged in a rectangular grid the area of a New York City square block. Some of the steles were three feet high, others ranged up to fifteen feet. None had inscriptions, only a blankness where I expected something. No Holocaust victims were named, none of their stories were told. There was an oppressive air of sadness and loss, but you had to work to pick out the doomsday vibe of the Holocaust.

I could see the outer edge of any row I was in, but upon reaching it I had no sense that I had arrived at a destination. There was always another row to walk down, and another row after that. As I passed some of the taller steles, the surrounding neighborhood disappeared from view, disorienting me. Nothing to do but keep walking till I had enough of walking. Forty-five minutes later I still was uncertain how the memorial was a statement about the Holocaust.

I was mulling this over when, rounding a corner, I almost bumped into a couple wearing cutoff jeans and Go-Gator T-shirts, the guy photographing the girl, who was grinning clownishly as she peeked out from behind one of the steles. My instinct was to tell them, "Hey, this is a memorial, show some respect. Stop fooling around."

But I stayed silent. I had just a minute before admitted my uncertainty about the memorial's meaning. How could I say this couple's fooling around was over the line when there was no clear line? If they wanted to treat the memorial as a playground, there was nothing I could point to in order to show they had gotten it wrong.

Jews in the millions murdered. Families shattered, traditions desecrated. Shouldn't a Holocaust memorial acknowledge these facts in a way that can be easily grasped? Do you have to decipher a Holocaust memorial before its meaning is clear? But what I knew about the pedigree of the memorial suggested that the uncertainty I felt was intended.

Peter Eisenman, who designed the memorial, has declared his affinity for deconstruction, a mode of thinking that spread, seemingly unstoppably, through academic circles in the 1970s. Deconstruction holds that there is no single truth. It uses terms like "the free play of meanings" and argues that coherence is a false ideal. Eisenman built ambiguity, which deconstruction insists on, into the steles of his Berlin memorial.

I descended the steps to the information center. It had not been in Eisenman's original design but was added later at the insistence of the local organizing commission as an antidote to the memorial's puzzling austerity. A young woman checked my rain poncho and wished me a perfunctory good day, and I took that as a sign that I was back in the workaday world. Here there was none of the mystery of the blank steles of the memorial above ground. Indeed, one question that had troubled me there was answered directly. The Holocaust, which the memorial suggested was a tragedy beyond any earthly specifics, was given names and faces.

There were photographs of Jews being rounded up by the Gestapo, Jews at forced labor, Jews in the death camps. The biographies of some of the victims were spelled out. A Lithuanian businessman and his four sons all killed in Treblinka. A Polish farmer and his family of seven buried in a mass grave near Lodz. Particular lives, various nationalities. But it struck me that the exhibit actually argued against individual destiny. All the stories led to the same ending—it made it seem that the way it was, was the way it had to be.

This depiction of the Nazi killing machine at work was depressing. I was left in awe of the implacable power of evil. All of which made me appreciate, as I hadn't before, the ambiguous story told by the memorial. At least it didn't just repeat history as it had been written by the Nazis.

Walking through the exhibit, I found it impossible not to think of the members of the Ripp family who had been killed. Viewed from one angle, their fate seemed controlled by the same iron logic that seemed to control the fate of the Jews shown in the photographs. For them also, the sequence of events that led to their murder was locked into place. But was the way that it was really the way it had to be? Over the years, I had toyed with that question, but I resisted considering it at length. What was the point of worrying about what was over and done long ago? But now in the information center, that question nagged at me again. Was there a particular missed turn that had sent Alexandre and the other members of the Ripp family down the path to their death while the Kahan family had found a detour to safety?

The next day I took the U-Bahn to Bayerische Viertel, a neighborhood in the outlying western part of Berlin. I had been told there was a Holocaust memorial there that I might find interesting, and I had arranged to meet with its creators, Renata Stih and Frieder Schnock.

I got to the appointed spot early, which gave me time to glance at a billboard that had a brief history of the neighborhood. It had once been called Jewish Switzerland, because of the numerous Jewish residents. Einstein had lived here, so had the psychoanalyst Erich Fromm and the director Erwin Piscator and some sixteen thousand other Jews. Six thousand died in the camps. Others were lucky to have made it out before the Nazi extermination machine was fully in gear. Now there were not enough Jews left to call the neighborhood Jewish Switzerland or Jewish anything.

There was still some time to spare and I decided to have a look around. Several streets radiated off a plaza, and I set off at random. It was a middle-class neighborhood, sedate to the point of somnolence. There were few pedestrians on the tree-lined, cobblestoned streets. Several outdoor cafés with more sparrows than patrons. Four- and five-story stucco row houses, some with shades drawn though it was getting on to noon. But no Holocaust memorial.

As I turned a corner, I noticed a two-by-three-foot sign affixed to a lamppost at a height of fifteen feet or so. I almost missed it, it was so unobtrusive. On one side there was a pictogram of a chalked hopscotch game. On the reverse side, a line of text. *Arischen und nichtarischen Kindern wird das Spielen miteinander untersagt* (Aryan and non-Aryan children are forbidden from playing together). On the next street, another sign, this one with a pictogram of swimming trunks. On the reverse side again some text: *Jews can no longer use Berlin pools.* On the alert now, I noticed the signs more frequently. A pictogram of a chessboard and the sentence *Jews are not permitted in the National Chess Association.* A pictogram of a piece of music notation and the sentence *Jews are expelled from all choral groups.*

This was, I too slowly realized, the memorial I had come to see. If it was odd to find a memorial dispersed throughout a neighborhood instead of standing in one spot, the arrangement nevertheless made sense. The intervals between the signs mirrored the step-by-step corruption of a nation's soul that culminated in the view that murdering Jews was acceptable.

When I returned to the U-Bahn station, Renata and Frieder had just arrived. Both were somewhere in their fifties, was my guess. She was voluble, he was reticent. She was short, he was close to six feet. She was demonstrative, emphasizing with gestures her outrage at Nazi behavior. He rolled his eyes at each of her examples, indicating his disgust. We set off on our tour of the neighborhood, Renata in the lead.

She said, "When we first put up the signs, some people took them to be new government rules. There were calls to the police asking when they would go into effect. Apparently these people believed that it was perfectly reasonable for Nazi policies to be put back into practice. Finally, we had to attach a small disk to each sign to tell people that they were looking at art."

We came to a sign with a pictogram of a cat on one side and a statement that Jews could no longer keep pets.

I said that it must have taken a truly cruel imagination to think up such a rule.

"Cruel but ingenious," said Renata. "Pets can mean a lot to people. One man could not bear to part with his canary. He hid it on the balcony but a neighbor reported him. He was told to present himself to Gestapo headquarters. After three weeks, his wife got a notice that she should come and pick up his body."

We moved on. A sign with a pictogram of an ashtray: *Jews can no longer purchase cigarettes or cigars.* Another sign with a pictogram of a thermometer: *Jewish doctors can no longer practice.*

Renata said, "Just your everyday life. Petty things."

Frieder said, "It's because they were petty that they were so dangerous. A Jew could never be certain he wasn't breaking some law or other. Just crossing the street against the light could result in a trip to the Gestapo."

We stopped at a sign indicating Einstein's former residence. Renata said there was also an apartment directly across the street that he used for extramarital affairs. No sign for that, she remarked. The oppression I felt momentarily lifted. Einstein's wayward behavior was no reason to stand up and cheer, but it was a reminder that there was a time when Jews in Germany did not suffer awful consequences for every social misstep.

Coming round a corner, I noticed one last Stih and Schnock sign. Its all-black face was a perfect complement to the text on the reverse side: *Emigration for Jews is forbidden.* The last exit door slammed shut. The moment when the Nazis decided that making life difficult for Jews was not sufficient. They had to be kept nearby so that they could be killed.

Renata and Frieder had a favorite restaurant in the neighborhood, and after an hour of walking about we were all ready for lunch. The hearty native cuisine was accompanied by more wine than I was used to having at midday, and by dessert I was ready to sit back and listen to Renata's engaging nonstop talk. She ranged widely, from her admiration of Disney artists to the philistinism of American universities to Japanese men's obsession with German spas and the unisex Jacuzzis where nakedness was the rule.

"It's the implants that really get them, they love how they float."

I laughed because I found this funny, but I was also taken aback. Wasn't it too soon after our encounter with Nazi malevolence for even mildly salacious anecdotes? But how likely was it that Renata was oblivious of the circumstances? The memorial she and Frieder had designed showed a fine appreciation of the Jewish tragedy. Maybe what first seemed a tasteless remark was actually a proclamation of a belief—Nazis should not be granted the posthumous power to ruin the pleasures of the day.

How long after seeing a Holocaust memorial before life snaps back to normal? Several hours? A day? Each person makes his or her own schedule, and Renata had made hers.

On the U-Bahn going back to my hotel, I recalled how Frieder had summed up the idea behind his and Renata's memorial. "We wanted to make visible the conditions which led in an insidi-ously logical way to the destruction of the Jewish inhabitants." Yes, the Nazis had gone about their nasty business with a cold logic, tightening the vise by degrees. But what, I wondered, about the other term in the equation? Not the victimizers but the vic-tims. Darkness fell gradually—was it so hard to see that the clock was ticking and that it soon would be too late?

How was it, to put it in terms that most interested me, that my uncle Aronchik, Alexandre's father, didn't read the signs cor-rectly? France was not Germany. Nazi policies were adapted to fit different cultural and political circumstances. But the same ques-tion could have been asked about how Jews behaved in both coun-tries: Why was it so hard to realize that catastrophe was closing in?

What I knew about Aronchik's life in France was what my parents had told me, but they hadn't told me all that much. It was as if the arrest of his family colored all the facts of Aronchik's life leading to that fateful moment, rendering them unspeakable. But by reading about France in those years, I was able to piece together a narrative. There were moments when I had to stretch the avail-able information to cover some gaps, but this was as close to what happened as I was likely to get.

By the time he arrived in Paris in 1932, Aronchik had been badly treated by Poles, Russians, and Germans, sometimes as government policy, often in random encounters. The degree of mistreatment varied. But the cause was always that Aronchik was a Jew.

By comparison, France appeared a haven. French politicians routinely invoked the egalitarian values of the 1789 revolution. The universal rights of man, including equal rights for Jews, were enshrined in public discourse. Schools, now that their Catholic bias was banned, no longer smuggled anti-Semitism into the curriculum. Several years after Aronchik arrived, France got a

Jewish prime minister. Aronchik didn't follow French politics closely, but it surely must have pleased him to have someone named Léon Blum at the head of the government.

Aronchik hoped to become a citizen of his new home. He applied to the local prefecture, but the process proved trickier than he expected. Though some requirements, such as years of residence, were spelled out, each prefect retained a large measure of discretion. Granting citizenship was not only a legal issue. It also was an invitation to join an ideal community, one that allegedly existed in the hearts and minds of every Frenchman and Frenchwoman. Aronchik's petition was denied.

As war worries took hold, the anti-Semitism that appeared to have vanished from France's daily life turned out to have only gone into remission. Jewish workers were charged with warmongering. Rothschild the banker was caricatured as Rothschild the greedy, hook-nosed financier. Léon Blum's policies were denounced as "Jew policies." As much as possible, Aronchik ignored all that. With his wife Vera and two-year-old Alexandre, he had recently moved, and his new apartment on Square La Fontaine could serve as a symbol of his state of mind.

When I was in Paris recently and went to have a look, at first I walked right by Square La Fontaine without noticing the turn-off. When I doubled back, I was confronted by an iron fence designed to block the curious passerby. I got inside only because a young woman buzzed herself in and didn't notice that I followed in her wake. And then, lacking the necessary code, I couldn't unlock the gate to get back out. A resident who came by eyed me with suspicion before opening the gate and ushering me back into the city. It was just ten or so nondescript five-story apartment buildings on each side of a narrow street, but I felt as if I had violated a sanctuary.

For Aronchik and his family, Square La Fontaine could also

have felt like a sanctuary, off the beaten track and largely cut off from the life of the city. It was in the Sixteenth Arrondissement, and even during the German occupation, Aronchik could convince himself that his life would go on largely undisturbed. German patrols were most active on the Left Bank, especially in the immigrant districts where there were still pockets of resistance. Some Wehrmacht officers, attracted by the quiet and elegance, requisitioned apartments in the Sixteenth, but in general Aronchik could get through the day without a single hostile encounter with a German soldier.

After the initial panic, much of Paris settled back into routine, even though it was a routine suffused with the smell of defeat. Swastika flags were everywhere, to remind Parisians who had won and who had lost. But many normal activities were permitted, even encouraged. The Germans did not want to expend manpower maintaining a repressive occupation when the Eastern Front was in need of troops.

Aronchik had started a business, producing stencils for office use, and it was doing so well that he and Vera spent generously on new furniture. That investment would pay off in the long run, they told themselves, which shows they believed in the long run. The political skies had turned gray, but it seemed a perpetual gray, a gray that would hold.

In October 1940, city newspapers carried an announcement summoning all Parisian Jews to their local police station to register. There was little reason to suspect anything sinister—these were French police, after all. Ninety percent of Parisian Jews registered, providing name, address, nationality, and occupation. Aronchik was among them.

In May 1941, the French police, relying on information collected during the registration, summoned some four thousand

Polish Jewish émigrés to their local police station, where they were immediately arrested and transported to internment camps outside Paris. In August 1941, there was a more aggressive roundup, again relying on information collected during registration. The French police, acting under German supervision, blocked off the roads leading out of the Eleventh Arrondissement and took five thousand residents into custody.

Despite these ominous signs, Aronchik could still convince himself he was not in danger. In the May roundup, almost all those arrested were poor and without livelihood. Aronchik ran a thriving business. Many of those arrested in the August roundup were Jews, but most were also Communists. Maybe it was politics, not religion, that was the black mark. Aronchik was not politically active, and communism especially had no appeal for him. The gray, Aronchik could tell himself, was still holding.

But on July 16, 1942, Aronchik's world turned to darkest black. He was in his office when he received a call from a friend warning him that there would be a roundup of Jews that evening. Previous roundups had targeted only adult males. Assuming this would be true again, Aronchik hurried back to Square La Fontaine and hid in a vacant apartment one floor above his own. His wife, mother-in-law, and Alexandre remained in the apartment below.

From a dining room window, Aronchik had a good sight line onto the street. He watched helplessly as a van arrived and the French police took away his wife. His mother-in-law assumed that the very young and the very old would not be bothered, and she didn't take Alexandre and go into hiding. But later that night, the police returned and took both into custody. Aronchik never saw any of them again.

Aronchik had loved France, he had hoped to become a citizen.

France was a safe harbor after the rough crossings in Russia, Poland, and Germany. Aronchik believed those slogans about Liberty, Equality, Fraternity. France, after all, was the home of the Declaration of the Rights of Man. After the July roundup, he felt not only grief but also betrayal.

It turned out that the Rights of Man meant the Rights of Some Men, as defined in the small print. That was where you could see how France fine-tuned its conscience. The French police distinguished between native and foreign-born Jews. The former were part of the eternal French ideal, the latter not so much, and could be sent off to concentration camps with few qualms. And even when the Germans began deporting native-born Jews, the French offered little resistance. A long-standing belief, often made explicit in the 1930s, was that all Jews in France, whatever their lineage, constituted a group apart. In fact, the deportation that sparked the most public anger and was most resisted by the puppet Vichy government was that of non-Jewish French males who were conscripted for forced labor in Germany. Though that was hard time, it wasn't the death camps. But those deportees were purely French.

Aside from those he encountered through his business, Aronchik had met few natives since his arrival in France. He was never invited to a traditional Sunday dinner *en famille*, he never saw the inside of a French home. Aronchik never got a *feel* for French life. He could see what was immediately in front of him, the overarching dynamics of French life remained hidden. Aronchik had noted many ominous signs, but he was still surprised by the disaster that overtook his family.

The day after seeing Renata and Frieder's installation in Bayerische Viertel, I went to have a look at the Kahans' former apartment in Berlin. It was in the Charlottenburg district. Back then, in the 1920s and early 1930s, everyone called it Charlottengrad because so many Russian émigrés had settled there. Scheunen-viertel was where the poor émigrés lived. Charlottengrad was for the well-off.

The Kahans had made their money in Russia by producing and transporting oil, operating mainly out of Baku and Saratov, and they had been very successful. That part of the business had disappeared in the Soviet whirlwind, but there were outposts in several European cities to take up the slack. The Kahans pros-pered enough for them to buy an apartment on fashionable Schlüterstrasse.

When I came by, the apartment happened to be between tenants, and I persuaded the landlord to let me in for a quick walk-through. Opening the door and stepping aside to let me pass, pride of possession crept into his voice. "One hundred fifty square meters. This is a big apartment, you won't find many this big."

It was big, and luxurious besides. Eighteen-foot ceilings, wainscoting, elaborate moldings. Pocket doors with glazed glass. Off a twenty-five-foot corridor, there were six bedrooms. Also quarters for servants. The centerpiece was the *Berlin zimmer*, typ-ical for the architecture of the period. This large anteroom could hold the seventy guests who typically came to celebrate the High Holy Days with the Kahans. At other times, it served as a salon that attracted Berlin's prominent Jewish intellectuals and politicians. Family reminiscences suggested a place that vibrated with social energy. But then the Kahans decided they had to give it up.

In April 1933, three months after Hitler became chancellor, the Kahan family gathered in the Schlüterstrasse apartment. Since the death of the patriarch, Chaim Kahan, the family settled important matters communally. There were ominous signs that suggested it was time to pack up and leave Germany, but the

Kahans had already been forced from one home, in Russia. It was difficult to believe they would now have to give up the life they had built in Berlin.

The Kahans had come to Berlin in 1920, part of an influx of Russians who left or were pushed out of their homeland by the revolution. The émigré world was self-contained, almost self-sustaining. There were Russian theaters, bookstores, doctors, and lawyers. If you preferred, there were Russian hairdressers. Many émigrés never bothered to learn German. There were numerous Russian newspapers, scores of Russian publishing houses, cafés where you ordered your coffee in Russian or in the Yiddish that some of the émigrés brought with them from their shtetls. The Romanisches Café near the Kaiser Wilhelm Memorial Church was a favorite gathering place. It was daily given over to passionate debates about those events back in Russia that had caused the debaters to end up in this smoky Berlin café.

Those émigrés who did pay attention to their German surroundings often did so with contempt. The mythic Russian soul had best keep its distance or risk contamination. Russian culture, which the émigrés claimed to have taken with them when they left home, could easily wither in this coarse atmosphere. Vladimir Nabokov, who was part of this emigration, was skeptical about grand notions like the Russian soul, but his story "Cloud, Castle, Lake" captures the prevailing attitude. A Russian émigré wins the prize of a camping trip. The other campers, all Germans, mock and humiliate and finally beat him because he won't join in the hearty bonhomie. Germans want nothing from life but beer and a little sadism on the side.

Many Russian émigrés considered Berlin a backwater to be endured as they waited for the inevitable collapse of the revolution, whereupon they could return home. "There was a phrase for it," my mother once told me. "*Sidet' na chemodanakh*. Sitting on your suitcases." No need to unpack since you'll be moving back to Russia shortly.

The Kahans saw things differently. Because of their money, they settled comfortably into their new home, but they had always preferred Germany to Russia. How could you like a country that permitted pogroms and confined Jews to the Pale of Settlement? That wasn't a hard standard to beat. The men in the family had been sent to schools in Frankfurt and Marburg, sidestepping the quotas on Jews that existed in Russia's educational system. Family vacations were in Bad Kreuznach and Wiesbaden. Almost all the Kahans were fluent in the language.

Also, as important, the family was incorporated into Germany's commercial life. The business in Russia had been lost to Communist expropriation, but there were major investments beyond the revolution's reach. A chemical factory in Warsaw, a textile plant in Lodz, a publishing house in Vilna. But the Kahans' main interest was always oil, and this was revived in Germany. At the height of their activity, the Kahans rented or owned thirty-five tankers serving ports up and down the continent. Six hundred storage tanks were spread throughout Germany, stretching from Oldenburg to East Prussia. NITAG signs, indicating the family firm (Naphta-Industrie und Tankanlagen AG), hung on the numerous roadside gas stations that were coming into vogue.

When I was growing up, I heard few regrets about financial losses. The family had barely escaped the Final Solution. Leaving behind some gas stations was a small price to pay for getting out alive. When wealth was mentioned, it was usually to note that despite having money, the family had only a tentative status in Berlin society. I once asked my mother if she'd had any German friends at her school. She gave me a look that suggested astonishment that she could have raised such an oblivious son. Even German Jews, themselves largely assimilated, viewed Russian

Jews streaming in from the East with an apprehension edging toward revulsion. It was a case where similarities were all the more reason to insist on differences. *Ostjuden* was a word that came with a sneer. My mother's one German friend, a Jewish girl, was not permitted by her father to enter the Kahan home.

And it was also true that the same business success that gave the Kahans entrée to elite business circles also counted against them. Because the punitive Treaty of Versailles placed severe limits on the native shipping industry, the Kahans were able to exploit a vacuum. One of their most successful deals was buying the Wilhelmshaven oil tank storage facility that had served as a fuel depot for German ships in World War I. The Kahans were feasting on German humiliation—or so it could seem to the natives.

All of which put the Kahans inside German society and also outside. This made them different from German Jews. The resonant image here is of those German Jews who won Iron Crosses fighting for the Fatherland in World War I, letting them believe they were more German than the Germans, and then were surprised when they were shuffled off to the killing camps. The Kahans were not like that. They were in the life of Germany but not of the life. And that turned out to be the right perspective from which to see how events were unfolding. They had a *feel* for the society in which they lived, such as Aronchik fatally lacked.

Several weeks after the meeting when departure from Germany was decided, when the family was already packing up to leave, an event confirmed the wisdom of their decision. My uncle Lolia, my mother's brother, was strolling down a street when a platoon of Hitler's Brown Shirts marched past. The Heil Hitler salute was not yet obligatory, but it was advisable. Lolia didn't mean a gesture of political defiance by not saluting, he was just out for a stroll. One of the marchers broke ranks, determined Lolia was Jewish, and thereupon slapped him in the face before quickly falling back into step with his comrades. It was the routine quality of the slap that made it so frightening. Humiliating a Jew was all in a day's work, something that had to be done even if it meant interrupting the pleasure of a self-congratulatory march down city streets. Within three months, all the Kahans had left Germany.

When I was walking through Bayerische Viertel with Frieder and Renata, we chatted about how difficult it was to create a memorial that adequately represented the Holocaust. The enormity of the event seemed to call for rare ingenuity. Frieder had mentioned a design that had been proposed but rejected for the Berlin competition won by Eisenman's Memorial to the Murdered Jews of Europe. "One artist, Horst Hoheisel, suggested blowing up the Brandenburg Gate and scattering the stones around the city. His point? The Brandenburg Gate is a symbol of a German identity that existed throughout history. Blowing it up would show that with the Holocaust the old notion of German identity had shattered."

I could see that Frieder didn't think much of Hoheisel's idea, and of course its extravagance ran counter to a sensibility that favored small signs with elegant pictograms that some passersby didn't even notice. But I was intrigued. I decided on a quick trip to Hoheisel's hometown of Kassel even though it was a detour from my itinerary. Several of his memorials were there, and I wanted to see what had been concocted by a man who thought blowing up the Brandenburg Gate was a good idea.

On the train, I read up on Hoheisel and his work. I learned that in fact he had two memorials in Kassel. I decided to see the more modest one first, as a way of acclimating myself to his work gradually.

Hoheisel had visited the local high school with a list of Kassel's Jews who had been deported to the camps. He asked each student to research the history of one Jew on the list—where he or she had lived, what their families were like, how they died. As many details as possible. A sheet of paper with the name and a short bio of the victim was wrapped around a stone and placed in a vitrine in Kassel's train station alongside the track that once ran to the Theresienstadt and Majdanek concentration camps. The full interviews that the students had conducted were entered in an accompanying notebook.

It is a common Jewish practice to place stones on the graves of relatives. I've heard several explanations for this. One is that the stones block the escape of souls into the profane air. That has a provocative mix of the material and the spiritual. But what was the point of the stones as Hoheisel had used them in his memorial? As far as I could tell, he had devised a symbol in search of a meaning.

It turned out Kassel had two train stations. My train pulled into the Wilhelmshöhe station and Hoheisel's memorial was in the Hauptbahnhof. I set off at a good pace—a walk after the three hours of sitting was welcome. But it was a hot day and the distance turned out to be longer than it looked on my map. By the time I got to the Hauptbahnhof, I was in a foul mood, and it didn't help that the memorial wasn't where my guidebook said it was. One thing you should reasonably expect of a memorial is that it stay where it has been put.

The track where the vitrine should have been was not marked as anything special. The rails were rusty and weeds sprouted between the ties and the track seemed to lead off to nowhere, disappearing in the middle distance as far as I could tell. This picture of oblivion was its own sort of Holocaust memorial, a marker of the lives that had been erased from history. But it wasn't what I had come to see.

I was about to give up my search when I noticed two men in work clothes at the far end of the terminal. Catching up with them, I saw that they were pulling a vitrine. It was clearly what I was looking for, and I mimed a question.

One of the men, fortyish, slight, affable, replied to my gestures in accented English. "We're moving it to a place where we can clean it. Bird shit. The vitrine usually stands where there is no roof, so there's always bird shit on the glass. No one takes care of it, so I do it myself. Part of the artist's job these days."

I should have guessed this was Hoheisel himself. No workman would have handled the vitrine so protectively. When I told him of my interest in the memorial he had created, he stepped aside so I could have a better look.

Seeing the real thing, I revised my earlier opinion of Hoheisel's memorial. The clutter of stones, some forty or fifty, seemed to me a compelling comment on how the Nazis had treated their victims—arbitrarily selected, coarsely handled, jumbled together with no sign of distinctions achieved in life.

I told Hoheisel that I liked his exhibit, but he shrugged off my compliment. He was more eager to discuss the interviews in the notebook. "Some were wonderful. They had such intimate details, so much feeling. People who read them are always very moved.

"There was one story in particular. The student interviewed the grandson of the neighbors of a Jewish couple who were ordered to be deported. In an effort to salvage some value from the disaster, the couple put their household goods out on the street for sale. The neighbors paid next to nothing, a few pfennigs, for the linen tablecloths. Years later, they told their grandson what they had done. They told the story without embarrassment, even with a bit of pride at having pulled off such a bargain. It wasn't as if they had stolen the tablecloths. They had nothing to hide. It was what was done in those days.

"But the grandson felt very guilty. He tried to find someone, relatives of the Jewish couple or maybe just friends, to whom he could return the tablecloths. But he was unsuccessful. He couldn't just throw the tablecloths away, he had to keep them, he had no choice. He had this reminder of his grandparents' bad behavior always in his house. Can you imagine?"

I could imagine, sort of. I had a similar story, a variation on the same theme—call it the power of household goods. In 1943, a year after Alexandre was arrested, his other grandmother, Aronchik's mother, was taken into custody. She was so sick that she never left her apartment on Rue Jean Leclaire. In fact, she rarely got out of her bed, and that's where the French police found her. When they came to take her away, she hardly had time to get dressed.

In 1944, almost immediately after Paris was liberated and it was safe to move about, Aronchik went to the apartment on Rue Jean Leclaire. The bedroom was exactly as it must have been on that night. The bedclothes were turned down as if his mother had just gotten up, the pillow still had the indentation of her head. The vial with her pills was on the nightstand. It was as if she had just stepped away for a glass of water and would return momentarily.

Which is worse? A room where personal belongings are strewn about and the furniture overturned by crass intruders? Where the closet door is open to reveal ripped clothes and scattered shoes? Where a half-packed suitcase suggests an escape interrupted? A room where it appears that a life has been stopped as if in midsentence?

Or a room like the one Aronchik entered? Where there was no evidence of an ending, where it seemed a nudge here or a push there and life would resume its course? Where the resident was gone, removed, but time continued to unfold as if nothing remarkable had occurred. Life here was a run-on sentence, with no punctuation to shape it into a meaning.

As I left the Hauptbahnhof I had this thought: Was my comparison of the two rooms an example of the brutalizing legacy the Nazis have forced on us? In what kind of world does it make sense to try to measure degrees of cruelty?

Hoheisel corrected me. Kassel had three, not two, of his Holocaust memorials. I had gone wrong, he told me, by limiting my count to memorials dedicated only to Jewish victims. The Nazis also executed some two hundred thousand mentally ill and physically disabled individuals whom they deemed "not worthy to live." Hoheisel's memorial was dedicated to the victims of the T4 Aktion, which was the bland bureaucratic designation for that wholesale murder.

Anyone who has spent any time considering the Holocaust is familiar with the argument. The tragedy of the Jews was unique. Their fate has to be set apart from Russian POWs, members of the Polish intelligentsia, political opponents, Catholic priests, and several other groups that were killed in great numbers by the Nazis. The Nazis believed that Jews were not merely to be killed— they were to be exterminated. Jews were killed for who they were and not for what they did. But the victims of the T4 Aktion were also killed for who they were, not what they did. They also were to be exterminated.

Most other times, I would have been eager to see Hoheisel's memorial. I liked his ideas about memorials, and the T4 Aktion victims certainly deserved to be honored. But I was looking for memorials that would trigger memories of the Kahans and the Ripps, and the T4 Aktion seemed unconnected with that. But Hoheisel insisted and finally I complied.

The directions Hoheisel gave me were more suitable to the countryside than to a medium-size city. Just keep going downhill, he said, you are sure to run into the memorial. The line of gravity was sometimes hard to follow through all the curving side streets and expansive plazas, and it took me a while to find what I was looking for. But when I turned a corner, the memorial came abruptly into view.

It was a poured concrete replica of a German city bus circa 1940, and compared to Kassel's contemporary vehicles it appeared a mutant. It was obviously different—it couldn't move, for one thing—but it was similar enough in its shape so that it wouldn't have appeared totally out of place in contemporary traffic. What had once happened was history. But it was a history that, the memorial insisted, still intruded on the present.

When the T4 Aktion was carried out, the windows on the buses were covered to spare the townspeople's sensibility. There had been complaints that it was unpleasant to have to see the faces of the passengers on the way to the gas chambers. The windows on the replica were similarly blocked off.

The memorial was sliced lengthwise into two. The resulting aisle was barely wide enough for me to pass through, sparking a mild spasm of claustrophobic anxiety. On one wall there was an inscription: *Wohin bringt ihr uns?* At first glance this seems a typical question from passenger to driver—"Where are you taking us?" But parsed more closely, it suggests life in a society that has descended into grotesque caricature. Buses look like ordinary buses, they circulate through ordinary city streets, but the route ends in a death camp.

I was at the memorial only because Hoheisel had insisted, but I was glad to have come. Though the memorial was dedicated to the victims of the T4 Aktion, it turned out to fit my interest in my family's history. One reason the Nazi killing machine functioned so efficiently was the bewilderment of the victims, who often didn't grasp what awaited them until it was too late, and that was the case whether the victims were Jews or those deemed mentally unfit. From what I knew about how members on my father's side of the family were murdered in Grodno, the question inscribed on the wall of the memorial could have been asked by any of them.

The German army marched into Grodno on June 25, 1941, three days after the invasion of Russia, and shortly thereafter the Jews in the city were forced into two ghettos. Life in the ghetto was given a veneer of normality. The Germans allowed a Judenrat to be established, putting day-to-day administration of ghetto life into Jewish hands. Jewish police kept law and order. A stunted economy, with shops selling easily producible goods like shoes and cigarettes, came into being. Jews were encouraged to believe that the ghetto was permanent. Ghetto life was bad, but it could be endured, and at least it would get no worse.

But in November 1942, the ghettos were evacuated and many Jews were transferred to a camp in nearby Kielbasin. Conditions were excruciating, but there were no clues prefiguring mass murder. There were head counts every morning, as if losing even one Jew would damage an important quota. The men were required to do calisthenics to keep in shape. In various ways, Kielbasin appeared a stopover on the way to a labor camp. But actually the Jews had already been marked for deportation to Auschwitz and Treblinka.

When the rumors began to circulate that the next stop would be the killing camps, the Germans damped down unrest by requiring the Jews already in the camps to write postcards to relatives in Kielbasin: "Being treated well. We are working, everything is fine." The strategy was always to keep the Jews docile and bewildered, never let them know the master plan.

I knew that the Grodno Ripps had suffered and died because of the Nazis, but my knowledge was only a collection of facts. Hoheisel's memorial, with that single sentence etched into the wall, tied the facts together. The fearful uncertainty that must have marked their last days became vivid, something I could grasp. *Kuda vy nas vezete?* That was the Russian for *Wohin bringt ihr uns?*

I had enough of trekking through Kassel's hot streets, so I took a taxi to the third Hoheisel memorial in town, which was in the plaza in front of city hall. On the ride, I recalled what I had read about Hoheisel's opinion of Berlin's Memorial to the Murdered Jews of Europe. He called it "a kind of cemetery."* And a cemetery, according to Hoheisel, was a place for remembrance. But an effective Holocaust memorial should be about loss, not remembrance. Remembrance is a numb endurance of history. Loss means confronting the past. An effective memorial, Hoheisel insisted, should make loss resonate.

Had he applied those ideas to the memorial I was about to see? These were the background facts: In 1904, Sigmund Aschrott, a wealthy Jewish entrepreneur, donated money to build a fountain in front of the city hall. Over time the fountain became a social meeting place and a point of civic pride. The idea that a Jew could have played such a prominent role in Kassel's public life infuriated the Nazis. They disparaged the fountain as the "Jews' fountain" and demolished it soon after coming to power.

After the war, the city authorities decided something had to be done with the empty space the Nazis had left behind, and they organized a competition. It was surprising that Hoheisel's pro-

*Horst Hoheisel and Andreas Knitz. "The Brandenburg Gate Is an Empty Place [Berlin 2003]." www.knitz.net.

posal won—it went well beyond the conservatism of most civic memorials. He specifically rejected the idea of restoration. Restoration would have allowed Kassel to believe that what had happened during the Nazi era could be undone by an architectural sleight of hand. But, Hoheisel insisted, there was no going back to what once was.

Instead, Hoheisel meant to show precisely what had been lost by devising a ghost of the original. He built a fountain that is a mirror image of what had once existed. The whole structure is deployed underground, out of sight but still a part of the city's architecture, like a bad memory that can't be completely repressed.

Even having read a description of Hoheisel's project, when I got to the city hall plaza I was perplexed. A slight rise in the pavement marked off a circle some twenty feet in diameter. This outlined the shape of the original fountain. Narrow decorative lanes ran from the center of the circle to the perimeter like spokes on a wheel. Some key dates were etched into the concrete— construction, destruction, a few others. That was it, nothing more. But presumably nothing more was precisely Hoheisel's point. The memorial was not meant to remind viewers of the fountain that the Nazis destroyed but rather to underscore the act of destruction.

At the center of Hoheisel's design was a grate, and I could hear the gushing water of the underground fountain. Hoheisel had arranged the pipes so that the water flowed into Kassel's sewer system, thereby implicating the whole city in the destruction of the "Jews' fountain"—and, more pointedly, in the deportation of Kassel's Jews, which the townspeople had acquiesced in or, in too many cases, actively supported.

One aspect of the memorial hit a personal note. The memorial was a reminder of the convoluted logic of the Nazis' attack against world Jewry. The Jews were weak, miserable vermin—

and yet they somehow had great influence on the culture. The missing step in that argument was filled by the rich Jew, whose wealth supported the spread of a noxious worldview. Though the immediate target was Sigmund Aschrott, the Nazi destruction of the "Jews' fountain" was a symbolic attack against all rich Jews. And though Hoheisel had never heard of the Kahans, his memorial served to remind me that they were a prominent target of the Nazis because of their wealth.

In fact, the Kahans were sometimes quite rich and sometimes only moderately so, depending on how the oil market was doing. But they were rich in Berlin when hyperinflation was making it difficult for many Germans just to make it through the day.

Here is a bit of family lore about life in Berlin: One afternoon when my grandaunt Marie was out for a stroll, a window display of famous Rosenthal china caught her eye. The family had been forced to leave behind its china of the same brand in its hurried departure from Russia. Each service included six place settings with numerous plates and cups in addition to a variety of specialized pieces—sauciers, pickle dishes, tart platters, finger bowls. Some seventy pieces total. After considering briefly, Marie entered the store and placed her order. "Seven services, one for me and one for each of my siblings." The purchase price was substantial but within range for a woman of means. It was the timing, done just to enliven an afternoon's stroll, that was telling. Marie spent money as a whim took her.

It helped that the family had holdings abroad that were shielded from the almost daily battering of the local currency. My granduncle Aron Kahan had cultivated a network of bankers in other countries, allowing him to invest knowledgeably beyond the borders of Weimar Germany. All this, of course, fit the Kahans neatly into the Nazi theory of an international cabal of Jewish financiers.

Having money made the Kahans targets, but it also helped get them out of the line of fire, not only in escaping from Germany but also later, when they departed from Europe altogether. They had the money for exit permits and visas, for travel arrangements, sometimes for bribes. What had gone out the door as a favor on an oil contract was now reclaimed in the form of a crucial official document. And as important as having money was knowing where it came from. The Kahans' business had always had an international scope, which prompted them to think of borders less as barriers than as lines on a map that had minimal force in the real world. All this helped get them to safety.

The Ripps largely lacked these advantages. It would be an exaggeration to say that not having enough money was why eleven members of that family died in the Final Solution, but it could be said that money was at least partially why the Kahans didn't.

The bare facts about how the Kahans became wealthy make for an improbable tale. A Jewish boy from a small village in Poland was the third-oldest male in the family and thus liable for recruitment for a twenty-five-year stretch in the tsarist army. An arrangement was reached with a family in Brest-Litovsk that had no sons. They would raise the boy, and in return he would marry their daughter. After the marriage—she was sixteen, he was three years younger—his father-in-law helped to set him up selling herring off the back of a cart. And forty-five years later Chaim Kahan was a major figure in the Russian oil industry.

His remarkable success must surely have owed something to Chaim Kahan's character, though in truth I'm not certain what that was like. The descriptions in necrologies and family memoirs are so hagiographic that they are hard to credit. The best evidence for me is a photograph. It has the date—1907—inscribed in one corner and a sepia tint that somehow argues for significance. It was taken on the grounds of Petrol, the oil company that the family owned in Baku.

Some seventy workers are aligned in four rows. Fifty-seven-year-old Chaim Kahan sits front and center. With his white biblical beard, his squared shoulders, and his elegant derby amid a sea of brimmed caps, he appears every inch the proprietor. In the background are some of the things he owns—a towering derrick, two barracks-like structures, a row of carts hauling large cisterns. There's a rusty overturned wheelbarrow off to the side. Presumably he owns that too. There's a rigidity to the occasion, as at a command performance. No one is smiling, no one is relaxed. Posing is a chore, an imposition. Chaim Kahan is the one who has required the chore, who commands the discipline. Everyone has fallen in line with his wishes.

Of course, even if the photograph captures Chaim's forceful personality—and I may be reading too much into it—that quality can't fully explain his success in business. A Jew in imperial Russia needed more than a forceful personality to get ahead. Circumstances had to fall just right.

In the early 1870s, Chaim began to trade in kerosene instead of herring. Kerosene was used for lighting in homes, and was often sold in modest quantities that a small-time merchant could handle. But in changing his merchandise, Chaim was doing more than simply substituting one product for another. Selling herring could lead only to selling more herring, but selling kerosene put Chaim in step with the transformation of Russia's commercial life that was taking place. Kerosene was typically obtained from oil. When it became clear that oil was much the more valuable product, Chaim Kahan was in place to participate in the new market.

In 1877 he moved to Vilna, where with a partner he founded a company for the transportation of oil. It was not a large-scale enterprise, but it permitted Chaim Kahan to move forward in Russia's complicated social scheme. That included fourteen ranks, four estates, and three guilds, each with privileges and obligations. Ownership of the Vilna business made Chaim a merchant of the first guild (*kupets pervoi gil'dii*), giving him the right to live outside the Pale of Settlement. He moved to Saratov and then to Baku, on the Caspian Sea in what is now Azerbaijan. At the time it was the epicenter of Russia's burgeoning oil industry.

That Baku had oil deposits was known since at least the seventeenth century, when Zoroastrians made the pilgrimage from India to the Ateshgah Temple on the city's outskirts. They were drawn by the temple's Eternal Fire—"eternal" because it was fed by the gas fumes that seeped endlessly through the limestone surface.

It was only when Baku and the surrounding territory came under Russian control in the early nineteenth century that oil acquired any commercial value. The newly conquered land, awarded mainly to court favorites and military heroes, was parceled out under a contract system, which gave owners four years of unrestricted use of the property. Extraction was from shallow pits, which wasted as much oil as it captured, but the owners, who could never be sure their contracts would be renewed, were not inclined to invest in improved technology. The oil that was produced, a kind of sludge, was used as lubricant, as grease for harnesses, and—improbably—medicinally. This provided a small but steady stream of profit, and the owners, who mostly lived in Saint Petersburg and Moscow and knew nothing about oil or business, were satisfied.

One anecdote sums up Baku's offhand treatment of its treasure. When a party of English lords and ladies passed through the city, the governor-general organized a boating trip in the harbor, which contained considerable oil runoff. At his command, torches were thrown overboard, and the Caspian exploded into spectacular flames.

The discovery of drilling changed everything. Now nobody was going to waste oil to please some English tourists. In 1873, the tsarist government ousted the absentee owners who did nothing to exploit Baku's potential, and put up their land for auction.

I've seen photographs of Baku in its prime. Wooden derricks dot the landscape. Since some of the plots are very small, the derricks are close together. The effect is of a forest—one ready to ignite. My grandmother, who lived in Baku in those days, gave me an image that I've held on to. "There were constant gushers [*fontans*]. People would sit on their rooftops and watch for the next *fontan*. Fortunes were made in a day." Russia's economy at the end of the nineteenth century was poised to take off into a new industrial phase, and Chaim Kahan arrived in Baku just in time to climb aboard.

Jews in Baku could own factories but not companies that got oil out of the ground. Chaim Kahan concentrated on getting to market the oil that others produced. At the peak of his activity, he owned a pipeline in Baku, a refinery in Saratov, between two hundred and four hundred train cars—I've seen different estimates—twenty-three petroleum depots, and two tankers that plied the Caspian and the Volga. One track of his delivery system, from Baku to Warsaw, covered 1,570 miles. He probably profited more from transporting oil than he would have from producing it.

By 1912, when new laws gave Jews the right to own oil-producing companies, Chaim had accumulated enough money to make a significant purchase. I found a remark about the sale in the standard reference work about the Baku oil industry. "The oil-producing plot belonging to Princess Gagarina, widow of the Governor General, which was leased to the firm of Tsitutov & Co., consisting of one hundred *desiatins* [about three hundred acres] is hereby officially transferred to the firm of Petrol."*

The bland bureaucratic language shouldn't hide the momentous achievement. From herring merchant to buyer of aristocratic property—that's an improbable journey. There had been some setbacks and the Kahan oil business in imperial Russia never was as big as that of the Nobels or the Rothschilds, but what Chaim Kahan did was extraordinary. He overcame not only economic but also political obstacles. Somehow the road he took was always the one with the rainbow at the end. When his path was blocked, his guile got him to his destination. There were enough improbable successes that the story of Chaim's progress in the world might best begin with the fairy-tale phrase "Once upon a time, in a far-off land . . ." And as in a fairy tale, it was hard to say what was a nimbleness that turned obstacles into advantages and what was luck.

In putting together this account of Chaim Kahan's career, I have relied on table talk at family dinners over the years as well as memoirs, contemporary newspaper reports, some official documents. There's a fair amount of written material to be found about the Kahans, a good percentage in their own hand. The family seems to have always had its eye on the future, making sure posterity got the picture right.

---

*M. Ia Gefter, ed. *Monopolisticheskii kapital v neftianoi promishlennosti Rossii (1885–1914)*, 672.

There's much less material on the paternal side of my family. It wasn't a writing family. Also, there were fewer of them, and of these, several died in the Holocaust before they had accumulated enough of a life to fill a memoir. The victims of the Nazis included Alexandre and his mother, his two grandmothers (one snatched from her Paris sickbed), and the eight relatives who were caught when the Germans captured Grodno. As for Aronchik, he was too traumatized by what had happened in his life to write about it.

My account may therefore appear one-sided—support for an argument that history is written by those who leave behind the most documents. But if it seems I have slanted things that way, then I haven't done what I set out to do. This was meant to be a record of two families who, though they often moved in different spheres, in the end constituted a single narrative, and detailing how the Kahans lived shouldn't push the Ripps to the sidelines. The value of Ripp family history can't be calculated just by counting paragraphs.

I kept this thought in mind when I got back to Berlin from Kassel and headed to the Jewish Museum, where there is an archive devoted to the Kahan family. It is housed across the street from the main building, and I made an appointment to stop by. The building has a modern look, all glass and reinforced concrete, but the mood inside is antique. There is a pervasive decorum, which I associated with a respect for the past. Letting me pass, the guard at the entrance informed me that visitors should not make too much noise. It was as if the slightest commotion would knock history off its moorings.

The chief archivist, Aubrey Pomerance, a transplanted Canadian, led me into his office, and for a few minutes we chatted about his work. He was dedicated but also somewhat jaded, years of experience having taught him the limits of what he could accomplish. "It can be tricky getting people to donate to an archive," he said. "Letters, photographs, what have you, people may not have looked at these things for years, kept them in an old suitcase in the attic. But when the time comes to donate them, suddenly they cannot let go.

"It's odd, but this need to hold on to items seems to get stronger the further you go from the origin. One woman I met was willing to donate letters from the 1930s that had been written by her parents who had lived in Berlin. But her children, who up to then had paid little attention to their grandparents' story, insisted that their heritage not be given away."

I nodded sympathetically, though I was myself guilty of withholding a family memento. When I got the letter inquiring about possible donations to the Kahan archive, I rummaged around and came across a notepad containing my grandmother's recipes for desserts prepared in the Kahans' Berlin kitchen. The assertive Cyrillic scrawl projected an aura of authenticity. *Iatsa pod Beshamel'iu* (eggs with Béchamel sauce)—here was a dish, especially as it was always prepared by the family cook, that defined a particular degree of bourgeois plenitude, and that made the notepad suitable for the museum's archive. I hadn't looked at the notepad in years, indeed had forgotten it existed, but for reasons I couldn't have expressed at the time, I decided not to donate it.

Aubrey led me to a cooled room with several rows of large file cabinets. He opened a drawer and took out a document. He held it as gingerly as a religious relic, though it was in fact a very earthbound item—a letter regarding the shipment of oil.

"It's from the Rothschild firm in Baku to the Petrol office. Confirming shipment," he said. "Just one letter but a piece of a significant story. Most Jewish merchants at that time operated locally, but the Kahans' enterprise covered a lot of territory. They even managed to cross borders at a time when nationalism was very intense. The archive is a gold mine for economic historians. But we have more than just business correspondence—intimate letters, postcards from vacation spots, necrologies. We have some ten thousand items. This is a very valuable and unusual archive."

I was proud that there was such a large collection devoted to my family. The imprimatur of the Jewish Museum seemed to certify a history of accomplishment. But I was also uneasy. The archive wafted a sense of completeness, of a past fully accounted for. But was it possible to reconstruct the life of the family piece by piece till you ended up with a perfect portrait? I was dubious that an accumulation of facts added up to a life story. I didn't believe that about the Kahans, whose path was marked by lucky detours and happy gambles. And I certainly didn't believe that about the Ripps. Even if there were a comparable archive with ten thousand items of Ripp memorabilia, these never could be arranged in a straight line ending with the Ripps' arrival in a boxcar at one of the killing camps.

I left the archive glad I hadn't donated that notepad with my grandmother's recipes. That meant there would be at least one gap in the Kahan family's wall-to-wall narrative.

I took the U-Bahn to the Friedrichstrasse station. There was a Holocaust memorial a half block away from there that Aubrey Pomerance had suggested I see. The title—*Züge in das Leben, Züge in den Tod* (Trains to Life, Trains to Death)—refers to the *Kindertransport*, the program that took approximately seventy-five hundred Jewish children to the safety of England in the years just before the war.

The figures of two sets of children, looking off in opposite directions, are situated on a fifteen-foot-long bronze platform. At one end a girl, maybe ten or eleven, looks up at a taller boy, presumably her brother. He's smartly turned out in knickers and a sleeveless sweater. He strides forward with determination, suitcase in hand. The girl, also nicely dressed and with neatly braided pigtails, carries a doll. The pair disconcertedly suggests the von Trapp family children, ready to break into happy song. They are about to board the Train to Life.

The five children at the other end of the platform are of various sizes and ages, and all of them are disheveled. Their posture and facial expressions indicate distress and uncertainty. An open suitcase lies at their feet with a broken doll inside—a symbol for a civilized way of life interrupted. These children are headed for the Train to Death.

Aubrey Pomerance had told me to take note of the Star of David on the coats of the children in the second group. He said, "It caused a controversy when the memorial was installed. The last *Kindertransport* left Germany in 1939 when Jews were not yet required to wear the star. When you're dealing with the Holocaust, you have to be careful to get every detail right. People have very strong ideas about the Holocaust."

Looking at the memorial, I recalled Aubrey's comment with some concern. By the end of my trip I would have covered a lot of ground having to do with the Holocaust and made a lot of assertions. How many details would I have gotten wrong? How many people would I have offended? How much criticism would there be of a Jewish-centric view of history or, worse, of insufficient empathy with the Jewish tragedy?

But then there was this to consider: In *If This Is a Man*, Primo Levi tells how his memory of a passage in Dante's *Inferno* helped him to endure the concentration camp. For this, he was attacked by several Jewish organizations. These critics found it abhorrent that a Christian writer should be the source of a Jew's spiritual sustenance. You don't have to read much of Levi's work to see his extraordinary capacity for compassion and moral generosity. He was in many ways a model human being. If Primo Levi could not escape criticism for what he said about the Holocaust, no one could.

Forward, I told myself, on to the next memorial.

The pedestrian traffic on Unter den Linden was of a Times Square density. It was one step forward, one step sideways, and even so I was constantly jostled. That quick exchange of glances that averts collisions on New York City streets didn't seem to work here. So I adopted the local rules of the road—straight forward, no concessions or ambivalence—and that got me to my destination soon enough.

The Neue Wache is listed in many guidebooks as a Holocaust memorial, but it fits the category only awkwardly. It was built in 1818 for the palace guard—*Neue Wache* translates as "New Guardhouse"—and later served for various military ceremonies. This means the commemoration of Jewish victims of Nazism shares space with the spirit of Germany's militaristic tradition. It doesn't help that the neoclassical style, with ten Doric columns supporting a decorative frieze, is similar to the kind of architecture Albert Speer favored. In fact, the Nazis staged some of their self-congratulatory celebrations here and on the abutting plaza.

In 1994, five years after the Berlin Wall came down, the government rededicated Neue Wache as the Central Memorial of the Federal German Republic for the Victims of War and Tyranny. That covers a lot of ground, and before going inside I stopped to read a plaque that enumerated exactly which victims were meant. Those who suffered in wartime, those who died in captivity or as a result of expulsion, the Sinti and Roma gypsies, homosexuals, the sick and disabled, those who died for their religious and political convictions, those who resisted the totalitarian East German regime—they were all swept into one capacious category. Though I almost missed it, Jews were also mentioned. One critic called the memorial an *"opferbrei"* (victim porridge).

The room I entered was some one hundred feet by one hundred feet. In the center, dramatically brightened by daylight from an aperture in the ceiling, was an enlarged replica of Käthe Kollwitz's *Mother Grieving for Dead Son*. Though the son is positioned on the ground and against the mother's knees instead of in her lap, the reference to Michelangelo's *Pietà* is unmistakable. Kollwitz dedicated the statue to her son who was killed in World War I, and that antiwar impulse makes it generally appropriate for this memorial. But only generally appropriate. How, I wondered, did the use of Christian iconography square with the commemoration of Jews murdered by the Nazis?

I didn't stay long at the Neue Wache. It was beautiful to look at and affecting in its message, but it didn't fit the purpose of my trip. I was looking for memorials that conjured up stories about the Ripps and the Kahans. Neue Wache offered no point of entry for such personal reaction. It generated so many complicated references that sorting them out took all my attention.

Numerous historians date the beginnings of the Holocaust from January 1933, when President Hindenburg invited Hitler to become chancellor. The United States Holocaust Museum, an authoritative source, has that time line, and there is a strong argument in its favor. That was the moment when the Weimar Republic began to slide toward National Socialism. But the emphasis on politics suggests a rational progression of events, which ignores the barbarism that fueled Nazism. A more telling date is May 10, 1933, when Goebbels gave a speech to a rabid audience of forty thousand on Berlin's Opera Square, declaring, "No to decadence and moral corruption!" and proclaiming, "The era of extreme Jewish intellectualism is at an end." His speech inspired the Nazi book-burning frenzy.

There's a memorial on Bebelplatz, between the State Opera House and Humboldt University near where Goebbels gave his speech. A plaque quotes from Heinrich Heine's play *Almansor*: *"Das war ein Vorspeil, nur dort wo Man Bücher verbrennt, verbrennt Man am Ende auch Menschen"* (That was merely a prelude. Whenever they burn books, eventually they will burn people). That remarkable prescience must certainly have something to do with the fact that Heine was born Jewish. A sensitivity to disaster was bred in the bone.

A four-by-four-foot plastic window is embedded in the ground, covering a shaft that extends some twenty feet down. The shaft is lined on its four walls with white bookshelves—bookshelves but no books, suggesting the world as it was after the Nazi mobs ran wild.

The Nazi book-burning campaign had a personal meaning for me. The Kahan family in Berlin had a substantial presence in the publishing business. They published Yiddish literature under two separate imprints as well as prayer books in Hebrew. They invested in Petropolis and Obelisk, two firms that kept the Russian literary tradition alive in the émigré community. Some of these publications almost certainly were burned in Nazi bonfires.

Bendet, the second-oldest son of Chaim Kahan, was the one who was most involved in the book business. He was a partner in several publishing houses and also owned a bookstore on Berlin's Kantstrasse. What began as a hobby soon was taking most of his time. Explaining his interest in the book business, Bendet said, "Our family has brought light to the world through oil. Now we will bring some enlightenment with books."

Maybe it was because the humor gave them a bright inflection, but these words seemed especially poignant. It was only a few years after Bendet's declaration that Goebbels unleashed the hounds of ignorance and darkness.

Though Chaim Kahan valued the written word, he warned Bendet not to become distracted from the family's main business activities. There were quarrels, harsh words were spoken. Chaim Kahan believed that in going off on his own, Bendet was endangering an important principle. When Chaim Kahan had started his business, the ideal of family provided an organizing strategy. Sometimes his business plan seemed to be to expand to the extent that there was a son available to manage affairs in a particular city—Pinchas ran things in Baku, Baruch-Tanchum in Kharkov, David in Berlin, Aron in Warsaw. Other relatives filled less senior positions. For most of its life, even when it grew to international dimensions, the business had only Kahans at the highest executive levels.

My mother recalled going to the Baku business office as a small child and each time wondering about the man working the stencil machine to make copies of documents. It wasn't his job that drew her attention. It was that he was, most surprisingly, not a Kahan.

This emphasis on family had obvious advantages. Family members did their work out of love and filial respect, as no ordinary employee would have. Lines of communication were always open. You don't have to make an appointment to speak to your brother or cousin. And in a family honesty prevails.

As patriarch, Chaim was fully in charge. He didn't just administer, he ruled. But there was a sense of camaraderie nevertheless. Chaim had married at thirteen and he was only sixteen years older than his oldest son, Baruch-Tanchum. When Chaim commanded, his sons grasped the nuances of what he wanted because it was like conversation between brothers. They all spoke the same language, held to the same values. Nepotism can be a bad strategy for a business, but for the Kahans it worked.

Yet there were problems. Organizing the business on the model of a family produced a fog of uncertain responsibilities and rewards. In a family, no one gets paid for doing the dishes or cooking the meals. In the Kahan business also, no one was paid a salary. Money was distributed ad hoc, according to a system that was nowhere spelled out and that allowed for no appeal.

I once asked my mother about this arrangement. She smiled a little meanly, which was uncharacteristic. Apparently the iniquities of the family system still rankled. She said, "Well, three or four in the family really worked. The rest just went to the office. But they still got paid."

As long as Chaim Kahan was alive, all disputes were held in check. Everyone yielded to the strength of his personality. But after Chaim died in 1916, disagreements surfaced with special force for being so long suppressed. Chaim had fashioned his family into a commune. But as often happens in a commune, when one thread is broken, the unraveling is hard to stop.

The Russian Revolution made things worse. When the Bolsheviks took over Baku in 1920, the Kahans lost a major source of income, and they had to reconstruct the business in Germany. My granduncle Aron did most of the legwork, exploiting old contacts and finding new ones, and he was spectacularly success-

ful. He was responsible for buying the section of the Wilhelmshaven harbor in Hamburg. He contracted to build a pipeline in
Palestine. He leased several tankers for transporting oil from
Persia now that Baku's oil fields were no longer available. He had
a gambler's mentality, and he was on a roll.

Aron believed that the business in Russia was defunct, and
that he had built an entirely new enterprise in Germany. He included some family members as a favor, not out of obligation. As
he put it in an unpublished memoir, "It was understood that I
was taking shareholders into my own business, the business established and honestly developed by my own initiative and knowledge and energy." But others in the family were not convinced.
They believed he was only putting the old wine of the Russian
business into the new bottles of the German marketplace.

The dispute was enflamed by the ambiguity of Chaim Kahan's
last wishes. He had indicated that he wanted the communal
spirit to persist. Any enterprise undertaken by any of his seven
children should be owned in common with the other six. It was
a noble idea, in the spirit of the family ideal that had always
guided Chaim in his lifetime. Unfortunately, he didn't leave a
last will and testament that spelled out his vision. Matters took
on the melodrama of a Dickens novel in which missing documents drive the plot to an excited level. The family could have
used a Mr. Jaggers, the lawyer in *Great Expectations* who under-
stands the dangers of mixing legal stipulations with passionate
dreams.

But if I had to decide between the bad caused by the Kahans'
adherence to the commune ideal and the good that it brought, it
would be an easy choice. It was the sense of togetherness—that
the Kahans functioned as a unit, that they made their decisions in
concert—that got them out of Germany before Hitler sprung his
trap. When the Kahans held that fateful meeting in Berlin in 1933,

emigrating was not an obvious decision. Some in the family argued for delay, wanting to see how events unfolded before abandoning the comforts and pleasures they had built since arriving from Russia. But though the family functioned as a commune, it was not a democracy. Two of my granduncles, Aron and David, held sway. When they said it was time to go, everyone fell in line.

No one in the older generation of the Ripp family commanded respect in the way that Aron and David Kahan did, and so there was no one who could have decided for the whole family that they would leave France as the Nazis were closing in. Lev Ripp, Alexandre's and my grandfather, was already sick when he arrived in Paris, and he would die of a heart attack in 1938. (He collapsed on the same day as the Munich Agreement was signed—a logically vacuous coincidence but too dramatic not to mention.) Lev's wife Eva, modest and retiring to begin with, suffered from debilitating depression brought on by the death in infancy of a daughter as the result of scarlet fever.

The family's center of gravity in Paris was in the next generation—Aronchik, his sister Sula, his brother (and my father) Solomon, who was always called Monia. The three of them lived together, first in a dingy Montmartre hotel, then in furnished rooms on Rue Jacob. When Sula married, Monia moved in with the newlyweds. Aronchik married a divorced woman of whom Lev disapproved, but the younger generation welcomed her into their circle. They went everywhere together: to the movies, on boat rides in the Bois de Boulogne, to cafés. The Ripps had no communal ideal such as guided the Kahans, but nevertheless they were close. An event from their childhood bonded them together.

During World War I, young Jewish males in Grodno felt themselves at risk. I've heard two explanations of why this was so. One, the invading Germans were likely to single out Jews for punishment. (This was Russian propaganda—Germans of that era were tolerant of Jews.) Two, Russians often mistook Yiddish for German and would execute the speaker as a spy, even if they were longtime neighbors.

In any case, it was decided that Monia and Aronchik, aged fourteen and twelve, had to leave the city. They trekked eastward, into the heartland of Russia that was still untouched by the war. A family contacted through friends of friends was willing to give them lodging and food, but, as it turned out, only grudgingly. Schooling was intermittent, and as new boys it was hard to make friends. Eventually, Monia and Aronchik moved on to another family, this time on a paid basis. Monia found a few odd jobs to help cover costs. Somehow they made it through four years to the end of the war.

When they returned home, it was as if they had risen from the dead. Sula at first didn't recognize her brothers. As she later remembered it, the two men she saw walking down the road toward her house seemed vaguely threatening, and she hid under the kitchen counter in fear. When the three siblings at last flung themselves into an embrace, it was sparked by a sense of the miraculous. The ecstasy of that reunion became the point around which they mapped the rest of their lives. They had been given an unexpected gift of time, and they meant to take full advantage of it.

When Sula came to Paris for the first time in 1932, my father borrowed a convertible from a friend, and he and Aronchik met her at the train station. They drove around town for hours with the top down, happy to be together again. Every boat ride, every dinner, every movie enjoyed together was both a rerun of that miracle in Grodno in the past and a voucher for happy moments in the future. They believed in that future with an almost religious certainty. When the Nazis forced them to go their separate ways, their dismay was held in check by the belief that they would find a way to join their lives again. It had happened before. Why not again?

My father escaped to America. Sula spent most of the war hiding on a farm in the south of France. Aronchik managed to elude the Germans in Paris. After the war, the three of them did meet again, as they had anticipated, but it was impossible to think of it as a happy reunion. Too many tragedies had intervened, especially for Aronchik. The memory of watching his family being taken away by the French police had made his existence a kind of death-in-life.

The Deutsches Technikmuseum (German Museum of Technology) fits neatly into its Berlin neighborhood of numerous small factories and workshops. From one perspective, the museum's main building, redbrick and with few windows, looks like a tenement writ large. It took me a while to find the entrance, which was modestly marked and off on a side street. In general, the message seemed to be: This is serious business, no need for frills.

I had been told this was the site of a Holocaust memorial, but my query at the ticket counter drew a blank, and I soon understood why. The museum is huge and has remarkably heterogeneous content, encompassing a startlingly wide range of Germany's technological achievements. There are exhibits about the history of Germany's textile industry, the country's role in the evolution of the printing press, its participation in the computer revolution. A single-prop plane is suspended from the lobby ceiling. One exhibit is devoted to beer. (This was Germany, after all.) I was at a loss as to where a Holocaust memorial could find a place in this grab bag of national triumphs.

An attendant eventually directed me to two huge connected sheds where some thirty locomotives were lined up side by side. They were arranged chronologically, beginning with the nineteenth century, to show the history of the German railroad system. Walking alongside the locomotives, peering into their exposed undercarriages, I felt I was looking at the entrails of behemoths that had once ruled the world. Very impressive, I thought, but how did this story of success and power have anything to do with the memorial I was looking for?

The 1938 locomotive was the first clue that I was heading in the right direction. Its nose was decorated with a spread-winged eagle atop a swastika. A sign noted that railroad administrators were among the few outside the National Socialist apparatus who merited a Heil Hitler salute.

The next exhibit, for 1943, was what I had come to the museum to see. It was a boxcar that carried Jews to the camps. The rough-hewn wooden construction stood in sharp contrast to the highly polished locomotives, and the effect was to suggest that the museum had suddenly developed a moral sense. Technological expertise, it turned out, was not needed to transport millions of Jews to their death. You could do that on the cheap. But that tremor of self-questioning was gone as quickly as it had come. The exhibits of the postwar years resumed the theme of Germany's engineering successes.

There is one fact about German railroads that has always nagged at me. I can't decide if it is to be filed under "morally inert bureaucracy" or "willful psychological torture," and I'm not sure which is more criminal. German railroads charged Jewish communities for the expense of transporting Jews to the concentration camps. Four pfennigs per adult per kilometer, two pfennigs per child per kilometer. If more than four hundred Jews were loaded on a single train, there was a discount.

On the way to the exit, I stopped at the museum café for coffee and watched the steady stream of entering visitors. A band of tumultuous schoolboys on a class trip, a beautiful young couple dressed in the latest gear, a group of middle-aged hausfraus in jolly conversation. I was ready to bet that none of them had come to have a look at the boxcar exhibit. Several times on my trip through Germany, I was made aware of my particular status. I was an American Jew who had escaped the Final Solution. At this moment in the museum café, amid Germans intent on their pleasures, that phrase came up in italics.

The #47 train from Berlin's Hauptbahnhof to Warsaw's Centralna Station makes the run in a scheduled six hours. It had a first class, which got me a nicely appointed six-seat compartment, and also a club car with a bartender eager to please. But half an hour into the trip, these pleasures began to lose their appeal. I was, after all, on a form of transportation that had a guilty conscience. Germany's trains kept the Holocaust in business, carrying their human cargo from all across the continent to the death camps. And there's that emblematic image that almost automatically comes to mind when thinking of the Holocaust—the train tracks leading to the gates of Auschwitz.

My cousin Alexandre was on one of those trains, and thanks to the Nazis' meticulous records, I knew his itinerary. On September 2, 1942, at 6:00 a.m., Alexandre was taken by bus courtesy of the local French transport system from the Drancy holding camp, where he had been confined after his arrest, to the Le Bourget–Drancy train terminal outside Paris. A telex signed by SS officer Heinrichsohn was sent to Captain Gerhard Eichmann in Berlin, indicating that Convoy 27 departed on schedule, at 10:00 a.m. Another document indicates Convoy 27 departed at 8:55 a.m., under the command of Sergeant Weise. I can't account for the discrepancy. But the notation regarding Alexandre's arrival in Auschwitz is the same in both documents. "Arrived 4 September 1942: Gassed immediately."

The hum of the tracks lulled me into a semi-trance that scattered my thoughts, and as the train rushed through the Polish countryside I recalled a photo of Alexandre that I had seen in a family album. It was taken close to the time when he was put on the train to Auschwitz—call it a "before" photo that would have no "after." He looks out at the camera with a knowing glance, though of course he doesn't know the main thing. It was that glance that always got me.

Could it be that the past erupts into consciousness most vividly in a mundane setting, like a train compartment? Maybe commemorating the past is most effective as a private moment instead of as a public transaction.

But then there was the argument in favor of memorials. How they incorporate single lives into history. How they make personal tragedy a part of a global catastrophe, thus giving some meaning to what otherwise would be incomprehensible.

The train kept rattling forward. A vendor came by with sandwiches for sale. The man sleeping across the aisle began to snore. The teenager in the window seat fervently manipulated her smartphone. My musings about public memorials versus private memories faded away as I dozed off.

The train pulled into Warsaw at 1:00 a.m., two hours behind schedule. The streets around the terminal were deserted, and I found a taxi only with some luck, beating out a drunken couple who lurched forward from the opposite direction. Once we were under way, the cabbie said, "Of course you were late. Your train was a German-Polish joint effort. How would that sort of co-operation ever work? We're supposed to forget everything that happened between our two countries during the war?"

The cabbie probably overcharged me, but I let that pass. I decided his comment was worth a few extra zlotys. It was good to be reminded that my border crossing was not just a geograph-ical transition. I had passed from a country that had been the aggressor in World War II to one that had been a victim, and that meant that the Holocaust memorials were sure to be different.

My friend Agata Tuszynska is a writer and longtime resident of Warsaw, and she has strong opinions about her hometown. She said, "If you want to see a proper Holocaust memorial, forget the one for the Warsaw ghetto. It's for tourists. Go see the monument to Janusz Korczak."

The manager of the B and B where I was staying was a local history buff. She filled me in about Korczak. Born Henryk Gold-szmit, he was a doctor who became famous in the interwar period for his books written for children. In the 1930s, he estab-lished an orphanage with an unusual organization—an orphans' parliament to write the house rules, a court for the orphans to judge their own, an in-house newspaper. But none of that was what gave Korczak his lasting reputation. When the Nazis con-signed his orphans to the Treblinka death camp, Korczak chose to go with them, though given the opportunity not to.

The manager said, "There was an SS officer at the terminal when the train was being boarded. As a child, he had loved Kor-czak's books so much that he was ready to intervene and save the author. But Korczak refused to leave the children."

Tucked away in a small, nondescript park, the Korczak monument is easy to miss if you aren't looking for it. The space around the monument was free not only of tourists, as Agata had predicted, but of any human activity. Here was a public monument that attracted no public interest.

I sat on a bench to have a good look. The Korczak figure stands toward the back of a pedestal, his arms embracing six children of different heights and ages. His bearing and expression capture his generosity of spirit, his saintliness. The youngest girl at the front of the group is holding a doll and looking down. Several others look adoringly at Korczak. Presumably Korczak deserved adoration, but I was put off by the way the children seem to be there only to sanctify Korczak. Hadn't they also suffered and died? Should they be reduced to props at someone else's apotheosis?

As I was trying to organize my reactions into an opinion, a swarm of young people came down the path. They were Canadian high school students, their teacher told me when I asked, here as follow-up to their study of the Holocaust back in their Toronto classrooms. They seemed, in fact, to have had their fill of the Holocaust—they hardly looked at the monument, instead laughing and joking, and they pretty much ignored their guide's commentary. I didn't pay much attention either since what the guide was saying seemed only to confirm what I already knew. But she ended with a surprise.

"Some of you may have seen on the Internet or perhaps heard the story of how Korczak volunteered to go to Treblinka with the orphans. But that is a legend. It makes for a nice story, and we can use some nice stories about that terrible time. But it's not true."

As the group headed off to the next stop on their tour, I caught up with the guide and asked her if the story about Korczak at the train station was a myth.

"It is all because of one man: Władysław Szpilman," she said. "In Polanski's movie *The Pianist*, Szpilman is portrayed as a national hero. After that no one argued with anything Szpilman said. When he wrote in his memoirs that he saw Korczak at the train station that day, volunteering to go with the children, that became the truth. But there are many inconsistencies in Szpilman's story—he got the weather of that day wrong, also the time of the train's departure. But you really have to know only one thing. The Nazis did not give anyone that sort of choice. They were not so generous."

Later, when I met up with Agata, I told her about the guide's remarks. She said, "It was chaos when the Nazis were here, so of course people remember things differently."

We were in the Blikle Café on fancy Nowy Swiat Street, Agata having brought me there to taste the best *ponchiki* in Warsaw. I didn't tell her that I preferred Krispy Kreme, not wanting to put a dent in her hometown boosterism. But I didn't let politeness keep me from pursuing a topic that I knew Agata had grown weary of discussing. I asked her if she meant to say that what happened during the German occupation lay beyond understanding.

Agata has written a book about that time, one controversial enough to get her sued for libel. Its subject is Vera Gran, a popular singer who after the war was accused of collaborating with the Germans. Several judicial proceedings ended inconclusively, but the label of collaborator stuck to Gran, in no small measure because it was endorsed by Szpilman. Gran didn't go quietly. She in turn accused Szpilman of having been one of the hated Jewish police who had aided the Nazis—and it was repeating this claim in her book that got Agata sued for libel by Szpilman's son. The case was ultimately dismissed, but the nastiness of the charges lingered in the public mind.

"My book takes no sides," Agata said. "It just shows that memories of that time can be very tricky. How Gran remembers it, how others remember her, how they remember their own role. Who can say what the truth is?"

So, to recapitulate: Korczak's nobility of spirit was certified by Szpilman, whose relationship to the truth had been put into question by Gran, whose opinion was given publicity by Agata, who was sued for libel for what her book said about Szpilman.

When I had seen the Korczak monument, it appeared to sit firmly on its foundation. Now in my mind's eye it had begun to wobble, pushed this way and that by bitter disputes. Holocaust memorials may seem built for the ages, but they can get caught up in messy local history.

The Korczak memorial honors his dedication to the children in his care, his willingness to give his life for a principle. But as I continued to think about it, another notion also kicked in—how in those days of always imminent danger, destiny could ride on a single decision. It didn't matter to me if Korczak had actually made that noble gesture at the train station. Fact or legend, the story struck a responsive chord, reminding me of what my father had told me about Aronchik's life during the Nazi occupation.

Aronchik generally relied on France's proclaimed allegiance to humanitarian principles to get him and his family safely through the war, but there was one moment when he considered another option. After he was safely in America, my father managed to obtain U.S. visas for Aronchik, his wife Vera, and Alexandre, though these visas were very hard to come by. America didn't want an influx of refugees and maintained strict quotas. But because most Poles were trapped in their country by the German occupation, the Polish quota, though tiny, remained underused, and Aronchik had a Polish passport thanks to his residing in Grodno when that city was part of Poland. He had no love for the country that had given it to him, but now the passport could be a ticket to safety.

It would first be necessary to get from Paris to Marseilles, where some charitable organizations, including the Quakers, still managed to provide passage to America. Marseilles was in the Zone Libre (the Free Zone), which was technically autonomous. The newly installed French government in Vichy tried to convince the world it would act independently of German policies, and in fact the United States maintained diplomatic relations with Vichy even after declaring war on Germany. But Vichy was also eager to please its German overlords, and occasionally even exceeded German demands in its treatment of Jews.

By June 1941, Jews had already been discharged from most civil service jobs. Now the Statut des Juifs blocked Jews from any role in commerce and industry. Another provision in the law had to particularly worry Aronchik: All Jews living in the Free Zone had to register with the police. Anyone caught without proper papers could end up in administrative detention, which in effect was a concentration camp.

In fact, some local and regional officials enforced the Statut des Juifs selectively, considering it unduly harsh. Even those officials who supported the law were hampered by its complexity. Distinguishing degrees of Frenchness among Jews—stateless, naturalized, native born—was confounding. The reaction of the population at large was similarly varied. Some would have turned Aronchik and Vera in to the authorities because they saw Jews entering the Free Zone as competitors for scarce food. Others disliked Jews, and that was reason enough to betray them. Still others sympathized with the Jews and would have helped as much as possible.

Aronchik and Vera had to have been very unclear about their

chances of avoiding arrest once they were in the Free Zone. But it may have been the logistics of the crossing that were most daunting. Entering the Free Zone required a permit. Lacking this, Aronchik and Vera and three-year-old Alexandre would have to sneak across the demarcation line. Checkpoints popped up at unexpected locations, some of the terrain was impassable. Only with a guide did they stand a chance. Friends told Aronchik of guys who would help for a price. Other friends told him of guys who had taken an exorbitant payment and then never showed up.

But even with a trustworthy guide, difficulties loomed. Alexandre was an obedient child, and once put down for the night he usually slept through. But what if he woke in the middle of the crossing? The likely solution, sleeping pills, made concrete what up to then had been abstract. Trekking through the dark night, relying on a stranger for guidance, hoping sleeping pills worked as advertised—all this emphasized the uncertainty of the trip.

Ultimately, the trip required more than just courage. Courage meant gauging the difficulties and proceeding anyway. But that kind of calculation was impossible regarding Vichy, which appeared an uncertain mixture of entrapment and safety. What Vera and Aronchik needed was blind faith, and that turned out to be a quality they lacked. They remained in Paris, where the familiar surroundings offered some comfort.

The Monument to the Ghetto Heroes, honoring the Ghetto Uprising of 1943, was created by Nathan Rapoport in 1948. I had already seen another of his memorials in New Jersey's Liberty Park, where I had picked up an informational leaflet that had this quote by Rapoport: "I wish to believe my hands are a gift of

God." Someone like Rapoport, with his self-proclaimed genius, shouldn't be allowed anywhere near a Holocaust memorial. But still I couldn't not go to see what he had created. If you are Jewish, you can't visit Warsaw and not see it. It's like synagogue on the High Holy Days—even the nonbelievers show up.

After a twenty-minute bus ride away from the city center and then a short walk through a nondescript residential neighborhood, I turned a corner and the memorial sort of hove into view, so imposing that it dared you to pass it by. It is thirty-six feet high, a two-sided construction, each side presenting a version of the Jewish character. On one side, seven heroically sculpted figures with Mordechai Anielewicz, the leader of the Jewish Fighting Organization, at the center. One figure holds a knife, another some sticks of dynamite. Anielewicz has a grenade. This was Jews in warrior mode, resisting the oppressor. On the other side, twelve forlorn figures, including infants and stooped old men with their eyes on the ground. In the background, three Nazi-style helmets and two bayonets mark the presence of German soldiers forcing the Jews along. This was Jews as victims, an eternally oppressed people.

I circled the memorial twice, scrutinizing it. It was an assertive piece of work. The style was ponderous, bordering on grandiose. Close up, I felt its oppressive weight. If a memorial were able to buttonhole you and demand that you accept its argument, this one would have. Jews, it so much as shouted, should have stripped away the passivity that had marked their character for centuries. They should have cultivated the fighting spirit typified by Anielewicz. If this meant certain death, at least it would have been a death with dignity.

Rapoport's memorial argues that Jews had to choose, but it seemed to me he ignored the fact that it was a time when the very idea of choice was in question. The memorial not only doesn't acknowledge the ambiguities that shadowed many decisions, it dismisses them as irrelevant. But in fact, much of the time, doing nothing was the best course available. What Rapoport's memorial fails to honor is the ability of Jews to maintain a sense of self even as the world collapsed around them. Given the odds, that should count as a great victory.

Years after the war, my father told me this anecdote: "When the Germans invaded France, Aronchik and I were technically still in the Polish army, though by that time the Polish army had ceased to exist. Almost all Polish soldiers were captured or dead. One day I said to Aronchik, 'I wish something could be done to slow down the German advance.' He said, 'We can try a pincer strategy—you attack from the right flank, I'll take the left. Keep up the honor of Poland.'"

Though he smiled, I guessed my father wanted to make a serious point. Yes, the fact that Aronchik didn't try to get to Marseilles had tragic consequences for his wife and son, but that said little about the strength of Aronchik's character. In suggesting a two-man campaign against the German army, Aronchik understood how little room there was for action. And in turning that circumstance into a joke, he retained a sense of self in a world gone mad.

On the way back to the city center from the ghetto memorial, I got off the bus at the wrong stop, and the walk to my hotel took me past a massive wedding cake of a building that was so incongruous amid the modern glass-and-steel high-rises that I stopped to gawk. This was the former Palace of Culture, a replica of the Stalinesque skyscrapers I had seen during a summer I spent in Moscow. In the middle of Warsaw, the building was a reminder of the post–World War II era when Poland was under Soviet control.

I should have kept that in mind when looking at the Monument to the Ghetto Heroes. The style is straight-up Socialist Realism. And though the memorial honors Jewish fighters, it also proclaims the proletarian ideal. It is no accident that the Anielewicz figure is front and center—his membership in the Jewish Bund, which had links to the Polish Communist party, makes him an excellent symbol of the ideology embedded in the memorial.

That moment in front of the Palace of Culture, looking at its anachronistic architecture, made me realize something I had only dimly grasped before: A memorial should be looked at through the prism of history. Politics change, the balance of power shifts, and so does the meaning of a memorial. If I wanted to understand the Monument to the Ghetto Heroes, I had to consider Polish history.

In the years following the war, the government used the memorial to showcase its pro-Moscow allegiance. The Jewish nature of the Ghetto Uprising was elided, the proletariat's battle with fascism emphasized. But as popular resistance to Soviet domination grew, the meaning of the memorial became contested, and the government shifted its position to accommodate the mood of the country.

The fortieth anniversary of the Ghetto Uprising provided the government with an opportunity to exhibit a new openness to the West. Numerous foreign dignitaries were invited, including from various Jewish organizations. A fair number showed up at the ceremony, which was marked by a military detail laying a wreath at the foot of the Monument to the Ghetto Heroes. The hope, apparently, was that a single gaudy moment could distract attention from decades of semi-official anti-Semitism.

Marek Edelman, the last surviving leader of the Ghetto Uprising, naturally disapproved of the duplicity. His letter urging a boycott of the ceremony was published in an underground newspaper and widely circulated in the West. "Commemorating our anniversary here, where today degradation and coercion weigh upon the whole of social life, . . . is to be disloyal to our struggle." He suggested a proper reaction to the sham celebration. "Far from manipulated commemorations, in the silence of graves and hearts, will survive the true memory of victims and heroes."*

Edelman's position constitutes a strategic withdrawal. Faced with a ceremony that corrupts the meaning of a memorial, he does not take issue directly, repudiating lies and advocating changes. Communism in Poland did not bend to argument. The honorable thing to do—the only effective thing to do—is to have one's own conscience be the site of memory.

Communism is dead in Poland as in the rest of the world. But other political forces can still control the meaning of memorials. There is a way around that unfortunate fact: It is always possible to reject what is in front of one's eyes and instead make do with an invisible ceremony enacted in one's head.

There's a Holocaust memorial in Warsaw that still goes by its German name, which might seem odd—why retain this evidence that the Nazis had so much power they could even abrogate the local language? Chalk it up to the desire to be absolutely clear that it was the Germans who killed the Jews of Poland. Enough people have argued that native anti-Semitism played a role as to make such a declaration seem necessary.

Umschlagplatz translates as "collection point." In 1942, a railroad siding ran by this spot. Three hundred thousand Jews

---

*Michael C. Steinlauf. *Bondage to the Dead: Poland and the Memory of the Holocaust*, 107–108.

from the Warsaw ghetto were transported from here to Treblinka. Today the neighborhood is mainly working-class, with
no sign of the crime perpetrated years before. Even the memorial
that I was looking for was at first nowhere to be seen. Though I
was walking on Stawki Street, the location indicated in my guidebook, I noticed it only when I was standing directly in front of
the entrance. The façade was flush with the adjacent building. A
small, dreary parking lot abutted the memorial toward the back.
Passersby strolled along without a glance. Only two guys who
were leaning against the façade while having a smoke seemed
to have any use for the memorial at all. The memorial seemed on
the verge of vanishing into its neighborhood.

The gray stone façade was some ten feet high and forty feet
wide. In the middle there was a gap that served as the entry. This
was surmounted by a plaque of reddish stone with a relief carving
of bent and broken trees. My guidebook said this was a depiction
of a shattered forest, symbolic of the destruction of the Jewish
people, and that seemed as good an explanation as any I could
come up with. In fact, the memorial had several features that
made me reach for my guidebook.

The back wall of the memorial was inscribed with hundreds
of Jewish first names, from Aba to Zina, an elegant way to give
biographical ballast to what otherwise would have appeared
an anonymous tragedy. My guidebook noted that there were exactly four hundred names. Each name stood for one thousand
Jews transported from here to Treblinka. The math seemed
fuzzy—weren't there three hundred thousand deportees?—but
that ambiguity struck me as making its own kind of point. The
transportation of bodies for slaughter was not something to be
calculated with precision.

I turned my attention to the layout of the interior. My guidebook said it was reminiscent of a boxcar that carried Jews to

Treblinka. I thought, well, yes, the dimensions of the space were about right, but the granite walls and the lack of a roof didn't fit. You had to make allowances to get the image to work. But even though the Umschlagplatz evocation of a boxcar was imprecise, it struck a spark—a boxcar had carried Alexandre to Auschwitz.

I have a copy of the manifest for Convoy 27, the train Alexandre was on. There were 1,016 Jews aboard, 752 female and 264 male. Some of them were children. Along with the French, the different nationalities included Poles, Hungarians, Germans, Austrians, Czechs, Romanians, Lithuanians, Latvians, and Dutch.

Alexandre's name in the manifest appears right above Nicolas Rittenberg, born on February 2, 1928, and two below Michel Reiss, born January 26, 1900. Most of the ages indicated on the manifest are between fifteen and forty. At three, Alexandre was among the youngest on the train.

The manifest describes Alexandre's ride to Auschwitz in terms of facts and figures, and that reflects the Nazi purpose. Before the Nazis killed Jews, they meant to dehumanize them, turning them into so much cargo. Reading the manifest, I could only marvel at how so many people were forced into a small area. Did Alexandre have room to lie down? Where did he urinate and defecate? Did being among the youngest mean less access to the little food that was available? Did the babel of foreign languages keep him from asking for help? I was trapped within a circle of merely physical information. There was nothing in the manifest that allowed me to imagine anything beyond basic needs and fears.

I left Umschlagplatz after another five minutes. The two guys were still having a smoke. The few passersby didn't pause as they hurried about their tasks. The cars with their honking horns that rushed along the broad thoroughfare a few feet away from the memorial entrance neatly symbolized that Warsaw's attention lay elsewhere. Still, I was glad that I had come. It had gotten me thinking about boxcars.

When I was in Berlin, I had gone to see the Holocaust memorial on Levetzowstrasse, which includes a boxcar. The memorial is on the site of what once was one of the city's largest synagogues. The Nazis used the synagogue as a collection point for Jews before they were loaded onto trains to the camps. Later in the war, it was destroyed in an Allied bombing raid.

The boxcar is one element in a complex installation. Metal plaques with reliefs depicting Berlin synagogues that were destroyed by the Nazis are embedded in the ground. There is a pillar engraved with the dates of the deportations from this site. A short section of tracks recalls the tracks to the camps. These elements point to historical facts, and together they suggest that the Holocaust can be put into a coherent narrative, a step-by-step account of how Berlin's Jewish community was destroyed.

But if you approach the memorial from an angle, the boxcar is the last element you come to, and it radically changes the story. The boxcar is highly stylized, its sides a jumble of plating that follows no obvious rules of design. It could refer to a myth of destruction. Certainly, unlike with the other elements of the memorial, it's impossible to think of the boxcar as pointing to something in the real world—and in this it constitutes an argument against merely historical facts. This boxcar disrupts any rational narrative that tries to account for the Final Solution.

The low-slung roof of the boxcar rests directly on the heads of the figures inside. Those who are about to die seem to be an integral part of the vehicle taking them to their death. It's as if, with the ending already foretold, they accept their fate and even assist in hurrying it forward. There are some ten figures inside the boxcar. It's hard to know the exact number because the marble pieces bleed into one another. Any sense of individuality is erased. The riders in the boxcar are bound together, joined in brotherhood even as they ride toward oblivion.

The Levetzowstrasse memorial did not help me to understand the details of Alexandre's trip to Auschwitz any better than I already did. But it did something else. I was made to understand the boxcar could be the site of a drama in which hunger and pain constitute only one of the themes. The Nazis wanted to inflict physical suffering so extreme that Jews would lose all dignity. In this, they wanted to make Jews less than human. But, the Levetzowstrasse memorial argued, in their ordeal Jews could achieve a sense of community that was preternaturally human.

Several months before my trip, I attended a reception at the Polish consulate in New York City, celebrating the imminent opening in Warsaw of the Museum of the History of Polish Jews. The museum struck me as a daring venture, perhaps quixotic. How could the often virulent animosity between Jews and Poles be contained in the decorous setting of a museum? Relations were fragile right from the start in the thirteenth century, when large numbers of Jews, fleeing persecution in France and Germany, began arriving in Poland. Political authority was comparatively decentralized, and Jews enjoyed a measure of self-government to go with a degree of economic well-being. But Jews were never fully integrated into Polish life, both because they were kept out and because they were content not to go in. Their outsider status helped to stoke an always latent anti-Semitism, and it didn't help that Jews often served as tax collectors for the nobility. But it was only at the end of the seventeenth century, when a series of foreign invasions weakened the bonds of civil society, that anti-Jewish feeling became pronounced and sometimes violent—it was during this period that Cossack raids on Jewish villages became frequent. For the next three centuries, though they continued to live in close proximity, Jews and Poles regarded each other with hostility and suspicion. World War II did nothing to improve relations, which at first glance can seem surprising. The Germans were the common enemy, Poles and Jews should have been comrades. But each had complaints about the other's actions, and these continue to this day.

The Jewish position: Ignore for the moment what happened during the war when Poles claimed not to see the killing camps right under their noses. Ignore also that some Poles denounced their Jewish neighbors to the Nazis. *After* the war, when the Jews who had survived the camps returned to claim their homes, they were met with pogroms in several Polish cities. *After* the Nazis left, *after* there was a return to normal Polish life, Jews were still at risk of being killed, now by their compatriots.

The Polish position: To provide more territory for the growing German population, the Nazis intended to rid Poland of its "racially inferior" Slav inhabitants through a policy of planned starvation. Three million Poles died. That's on top of the twenty-two thousand professors, doctors, officers, and other members of the cultural elite who were massacred at Katyn by the Russians. Given the suffering of the Polish people, why should Jews expect special sympathy? Not to mention that when the Red Army marched into Poland in 1945, many Jews sided with the Bolsheviks.

The two sides talk past each other, starting from different assumptions and moving farther apart as they go. At the consulate reception, the keynote speech by the director of the museum was an attempt to bridge the gap. "Yes," he said, "there have been unfortunate moments in the history of Jews in Poland, that must be admitted. But that should be viewed in the context of a shared destiny. There could be no Polish culture without Jewish culture and no Jewish culture without Polish culture. There was a time, indeed, in the sixteenth century, when people often said, 'Poland is paradise for the Jews.'" That harmony, the director insisted, had sometimes weakened but never entirely vanished.

I was surprised by this placid view of what I had always thought of as a war zone, but, I told myself, I was no expert. Present in the audience were the director of New York's Jewish Museum, the head of the YIVO Institute for Jewish Research, and a City College professor of Holocaust studies. I watched them during the speech. They listened respectfully, laughed even at the bad jokes, applauded at the conclusion. There was no sign of disagreement, and they were the experts. I began to think I had gotten it wrong, my perspective clouded over by family allegiances.

My father and my uncle Aronchik had spent their early adult years in Grodno when that city was part of Poland, and they had had a hard time of it—restricted educational opportunities, few job openings, and, on the street, bullying at the hands of anti-Semitic townies. They got out as soon as they could, immigrating to Germany. Though fluent in the language, my father always refused to speak even a word of Polish.

During the Q&A, the matter of Polish anti-Semitism finally came up. But the director had a ready answer. "That's not a topic for this museum. If anti-Semites want to be remembered, let them build their own museum."

No one in the audience objected to what seemed to me unusual curatorial logic, and after a last round of appreciative applause, everyone moved to the adjoining hall for drinks and hors d'oeuvres. An air of congeniality prevailed. But I couldn't shake the notion that the congeniality was really relief that the evening was concluding without contentious dispute. The new museum announced itself as a rapprochement between parties that had long been at odds, but, I had to wonder, could just saying so make it so?

I had been invited to the reception by the consul general, Ewa Junczyk-Ziomecka, though it was difficult for me to think of Ewa with that title attached. A week on Cape Cod with friends and family that featured long, lazy days on the beach and cheerful lobster dinners fueled by wine had dissipated the official aura forever. So I didn't feel bound by tact when Ewa asked me what I thought of the director's speech. I told her that I thought it papered over some serious differences between Jews and Poles.

She didn't let tact stop her either. She said, "You have the prejudice of many American Jews, thinking that Poles have a deep eternal hatred of Jews."

Would it have mattered if I told Ewa that what she called prejudice I called family history? But maybe they are the same thing.

The consulate reception was on my mind as I left Umschlagplatz and headed for Zamenhof Street. There was a memorial there that I wanted to see. The Trail of Jewish Martyrdom and Struggle consists of seventeen black granite stones of different sizes and shapes embedded in the roadside at intervals of about one hundred feet, all but one bearing the name of a leader of the Ghetto Uprising. Janusz Korczak gets a stone for his commitment to his schoolchildren. There is also a more elaborate monument that honors Shmuel Zygielbaum, the representative of the Bund in London who committed suicide to protest Allied inaction as Warsaw's Jews were methodically murdered.

The memorial was dedicated in 1988 by a Polish government eager for good relations with the West in order to secure much-needed economic aid, but the occasion also gave Solidarity, the labor union movement that was gaining popular support, a chance to express its contrarian politics. This took the form of assimilating the memory of the Ghetto Uprising to its own purposes. Solidarity's leader, Lech Walesa, proclaimed "the uprising of the Jewish fighters the most Polish of all Polish uprisings," a part of a national tradition of resistance to authority that now must include Solidarity. Walesa's words were an effective rallying cry in 1988, but it needs saying that they glided too smoothly over the rocky Jewish-Polish relations that existed in 1943.

The Ghetto Uprising of that year was so chaotic that it's hard to sort out motives and behavior. What's clear is that the main ghetto defense group—the Jewish Fighting Organization (ZOB)—hoped that the Polish underground Home Army would provide support for the Uprising. It's also clear that though some weaponry did get delivered, it was less than had been expected. The reason was no doubt in part ideological. Some in the underground distrusted the Communist-leaning tendencies of the ZOB leadership. But anti-Semitism also played a role.

Evidence regarding Polish actions during the Uprising tends to be arranged according to one's allegiances, and I admit to giving weight to examples where anti-Semitism can be inferred—my father's ill treatment in Grodno inclines me in that direction. So I fasten on the following: In its negotiations with groups inside the ghetto, the Polish Home Army favored the Jewish Military Union (ŻZW) over the ZOB. Where the ZOB was Communist-leaning, which the Poles abhorred, the ŻZW was Zionist. Zionism was the perfect solution to the Jewish problem that had long troubled Polish society: Jews would not have to be pushed out, they would leave the country of their own accord.

I started walking down the Trail of Jewish Martyrdom from the end where the "Tree of Common Remembrance" stands. The tree asserts that Jews and Poles endured hardship in common during WWII, and that notion is recapitulated in the inscriptions on the nineteen stones, which are in juxtaposed Polish and Hebrew. If different languages could express the same thought, then surely the people who spoke them sympathized with each other's destiny. It was an attractive idea, but sometimes ideas go one way and reality another.

When I looked at the words on one of the stones, the inscriptions remained just words, an exercise in translation such as might appear in a schoolboy's notebook. At the next two stones, the same result. Maybe for someone who already believed in camaraderie between Poles and Jews, these inscriptions were an elegant way to record that fact. For someone who didn't, the inscriptions were just words. Memorials, it turns out, are no good at making arguments.

I paused at a memorial stone on top of a small knoll with concrete steps leading up to it. A sign indicated that this was the site of the bunker that had housed the headquarters of the Jewish Fighting Organization, and that it was here that the leaders of the Ghetto Uprising had committed suicide rather than surrender.

There were two workmen tending the grass around the memorial, though they were more concerned with passing a vodka bottle back and forth than using their rakes. They were both blond and big-bellied, neat stereotypes of the Polish everyman. As I went up the steps, it seemed to me that they eyed me with hostility. And why not? To them I was a foreign Jew enjoying his tourism, while they were working stiffs catering to my pleasures.

The larger of the two moved in my direction, his fleshy face drawn into a scowl, and I tensed for something unpleasant. But I had gotten it wrong. *"Prosze pan,"* he said, waving me forward with that conventional expression of Polish courtesy, and I smiled and nodded in acknowledgment.

I had put up at a B and B on Smolna Street. It was just off de Gaulle Circle, renamed thus after the Soviets lost power in 1989. It seemed odd that this *"France, c'est moi"* guy had a plaza in the center of

Warsaw named after him. When I asked, I was told that de Gaulle had won Poland's affection by fighting in the 1921 war against Russia. Sometimes it can seem that Poland is still engaged in a rearguard action with the last century even as it marches forward into modern times. No wonder the country's Holocaust memorials can appear ambiguous.

Breakfast at the B and B was a communal affair, seven or eight guests seated around a large table. Each morning was a parade of national types—a Frenchman suspicious of the local cheeses, a trio of Russians as smug as in the days of empire, a pair of American retirees dressed as if for a day of sailing. Only the woman seated on my right was a blank, modest and unrevealing.

She was silent until I happened to mention that I had just seen several of Warsaw's Holocaust memorials. "For the best Holocaust memorials you must go to my hometown. Lodz has things you won't see anywhere else. Nothing compares with Lodz, I assure you." Now there was no stopping her. It was as if the topic had sparked some dormant wiring. She proceeded to itemize the features of each of Lodz's Holocaust memorials.

But I had no intention of going to Lodz. I had my fill of Holocaust memorials for the moment, and this hometown cheerleading only strengthened my resolve. Right then I didn't want to see another symbolic representation of the Holocaust. I wanted to get as close as I could get to the real thing.

It was evening when I arrived in Kraków, and the next bus for Auschwitz, some forty miles away, didn't depart till the following morning. The manager of the hotel that I checked into suggested I have a look at Kazimierz, once Kraków's Jewish quarter. The Nazis had destroyed the community almost to the last man, so after the war there were no former residents left to return to their homes. The neighborhood became a slum. But starting in 1999, there were efforts to re-create the look of the place as it had once been. What you got, the manager told me, was a Jewish quarter lacking only one thing—Jews. His tone was affable, implying no judgment. The world is what it is, that was his message.

Strolling through Kazimierz felt like being inside a very large diorama. Glancing through a shoemaker's storefront window, I saw the tools of the trade spread out on a table as if for the next job, but it was clear that the store was an exhibit and not a working enterprise. Signs on several buildings proclaimed their Jewish owners: STANISLAW NOWACK: SKLEP SPOZYWCZY (grocery store), BENJAMIN HOLCER: STOLARZ (carpenter). But it was all show. Stanislaw Nowack and Benjamin Holcer were long gone, likely killed in the Belzec camp along with the rest of Kazimierz's Jews. When I was asked for a fee upon entering the Old Synagogue on Szeroka Street, I wasn't surprised—this was not a house of worship but a facsimile of a house of worship set up to give tourists a sense of what the neighborhood was like before the Nazis arrived.

The restaurant I went to delivered more of the same. Heavy plush furniture, ornate silverware, turned-down lighting, and, to accompany the honey cake, a klezmer trio. The *Michelin Guide* would have given the restaurant no stars, but a theater reviewer might have found something to like.

My waiter hovered, talking up local points of interest. Serving my coffee, he said, "You know Kazimierz is where Spielberg filmed his *Schindler's List*. The events actually took place in Podgórze, a neighborhood that is on the other side of the river, but that was destroyed in the war. So he filmed it here."

I remembered the documentary-like look Spielberg had achieved with his black-and-white photography. I thought then that I was looking at Podgórze. But it now turned out what I had seen was a copy. Or, more precisely, a copy of a copy, since, as my stroll through town had shown me, present-day Kazimierz was itself a copy.

Auschwitz would provide a shock of the real, no more copies but the essence, and I looked forward to my visit the next day. It wasn't going to be pleasant, but that was the point. I wanted to look directly at the site where Jews died by the thousands.

It may appear superfluous since what was already in front of one's eyes—the tools of torture and death spread over five acres—should have been remembrance enough, but in 1957 there was a competition for a memorial to be placed on the Auschwitz-Birkenau grounds to alert visitors to the horrors that had been committed there. There were only two restrictions: No one who had collaborated with the National Socialist regime was eligible; and the camp grounds and buildings could not be disturbed.

Four hundred proposals were submitted; seven made it onto the short list. The winner of a preliminary vote was the Polish team headed by Oskar Hansen, who proposed building a black tarmac road, two hundred twenty feet wide and thirty-three hundred feet long, that would cut diagonally through the camp and preserve everything on its path—the barracks, the chimneys, the latrines, the barbed-wire fences. Everything that was off the path would be untouched and in time would surrender to the invasive action of grass and weeds.

Hansen contrasted his design with conventional memorials that he called "signs on pedestals." He argued for an "art as process,"* which would allow a visitor to Auschwitz "to walk through

*Katarzyna Murawska-Muthesius. "Oskar Hansen and the Auschwitz 'Counter-memorial,' 1958–59." *ArtMargins Online.*

the memorial, not around it." A visitor following the tarmac road would see close up the "mechanism of the camp" that had been preserved. But because what was off the road had been allowed to follow its "biological clock," the visitor would also understand that history continued after Auschwitz.

In the end, Hansen didn't get to build his memorial. The judges, not entirely persuaded by his unconventional approach, asked for modifications, which Hansen wouldn't accept, and he withdrew from the competition. But the episode answered the question, why bother to have a memorial at Auschwitz? Without a memorial, one sees the story of the Jewish tragedy only as it had been produced, directed, and choreographed by the Nazis. But a memorial is a chance for another way of looking. Hansen's proposed memorial showed that the death camp was only one moment in an overarching human history. The Nazis' time on the world stage, though horrific, was brief and passing. In the end, they lost.

The night before I went to Auschwitz, reading about Hansen and the 1957 competition, I was reminded of a memorial I had recently seen in Berlin. Conceptually, it was the opposite of the Hansen project. Exiting the Grunewald S-Bahn station in the outlying western district, I found myself in a quiet suburban setting. A busy pastry shop, a small outdoor café advertising a bratwurst lunch special, people walking their dogs—nothing in this small plaza suggested I was near a spot with a sinister history. But the Holocaust memorial, which was up a short rise and set away from the town center, was indeed just where it belonged.

Gleis 17 (Track 17) was for the trains that deported most of Berlin's Jews in the years 1941–1945. They were brought to this embarkation point after having been arrested and held at the Levetzowstrasse synagogue, and from here they were transported to the ghettos in Riga, Lodz, Minsk, and several other cities to the east before being dispatched to their final destination of the camps. Steel plaques embedded in the gravel surrounding the track note the date of deportation, the number of Jews on board, and the destination. There are 186 plaques, corresponding to the number of death train departures from *Gleis 17.*

But it was the tracks themselves that held my attention. The preserved stretch runs some two hundred feet, and as I walked up one side and down the other, I slowed to a ponderous, funereal gait. To go faster would, I felt, have been disrespectful. Jews on the way to their death had traveled these very tracks. The tracks were not exactly as they once were—the metal was rusted and weeds grew between the ties—but neither had anyone intervened to alter their appearance. Indeed, the tracks were not, strictly speaking, a memorial at all. There was no distance between them and the thing they signified. They were the thing. Maybe it would be better to call the tracks a relic rather than a memorial.

I spent a half hour, maybe more, staring at the tracks, and all the while thinking of nothing but these tracks and their lethal end point. No more expansive idea entered my head. Nothing about history, nothing about the effect of time passing, nothing about the need for justice—none of that could find a place in my thoughts. The tracks took up all the available space.

It took an effort to break the bleak mood that gripped me and to go back down to the little village square, where without a pause I sat down at that outdoor café and had a beer and bratwurst. The bratwurst was delicious and I savored each bite. How did the Germans manage to do bratwurst so well, nothing like the stuff I get at the corner deli. I even began to try to talk about the quality of the bratwurst to the jolly waiter till we both fell into laughter at my baby German.

Was it wrong to jump so quickly from thoughts about the

Holocaust to bratwurst? Had it slipped my mind that I might owe those Jews who departed on *Gleis 17* a few moments of reverence? But I needed to get away from the deeply unpleasant feeling that had enveloped me back at the track when I could do nothing but stand mute and powerless before the evidence of the Nazi killing machine. Bratwurst was how I broke the spell.

Auschwitz-Birkenau has been altered in several ways. What is now the parking lot at the camp's periphery was the middle of the camp in 1945. There is a reception center, which includes a cafeteria and bookshop. Crematory I, which stands at the border between Auschwitz and Birkenau, is a reconstruction symbolizing the four working crematories that are defunct and largely destroyed. There are other changes also, to accommodate the numerous tourists. But none of this hides the fact that a visit to Auschwitz puts you in the immediate presence of powerful evil. More than one million Jews were killed here.

I joined a tour led by an efficient young Polish woman who walked our small group of five briskly around the grounds. We passed the barracks where a thousand Jews were squeezed into a space originally designed as stables for sixty horses. There were primitive latrines, really just holes in a bench, in the center of the barracks where inmates were given barely enough time to piss and shit. I had a look at the punishment cell that was so cramped that inmates were compelled to stand for days on end till they died from starvation. Nearby was the wall where execution was a shot to the back of the head. All of this was hard to look at but harder to look away from. What exactly was I looking at? It seemed to me that what was intended to honor the victims was more an acknowledgment of the power of the masters.

We came to those notorious displays of piles of eyeglasses, of shoes, of prosthetic limbs, of women's hair. There was a pathos in the notion that once-robust lives had only these items to be remembered by. But along with the pathos I felt dismay. That the life of a Jew could be signified by a collection of parts seemed very close to the Nazi claim that a Jew was less than fully human.

At the end of the tour, as the members of our group went their separate ways, I caught up with our guide. In her remarks, she had of course mostly criticized Germany but also got in a few jabs at Poles for their actions against Jews during the Nazi occupation and immediately after, which surprised me. Most Poles I had met didn't offer much along that line. On the tour she had stuck to a no-nonsense tone, as if unwilling to provoke argument. Maybe she had already had some nasty encounters with Polish patriots. But now, after quickly gauging my allegiances, she was ready to chat.

Her regular job, she told me when I asked, was that of teacher in the local high school, and my query touched a nerve. "Our town is at the edge of a great historical crime, but I can't get my students to care. It's all music, the Internet."

I suggested that they had the excuse of being young.

"That's no excuse. If you are Polish, you have a responsibility to think about what happened in your country."

I was taken aback by her vehemence. I said that maybe they lacked a historical perspective.

"It's not that they don't understand, they don't *want to* understand. Sometimes I wonder if I should just give up trying." Her eyes, it seemed to me, were tearing up. It was just kids being kids, the usual classroom antics. Why was she taking it so personally?

We parted soon after that and I caught the bus back to

Kraków, but the encounter stayed with me. I was uneasy, even embarrassed. The teacher's connection to Auschwitz was many degrees short of mine, and yet she showed more emotion about what had happened there. Yes, I had felt grief walking through the camp, but I had kept it under control. I should have shouted, cursed, maybe screamed.

But no one did that at Auschwitz. The place dampened down anger in favor of dumb awe. You bowed down before the horror. That mood was built into the buildings and the grounds and the exhibits with their instruments of evil, and it was hard to step out of line. Even now on the bus, having left that circle of hell behind, those of us returning to Kraków with its fine shops and good restaurants sat quietly two by two, staring out the windows, in some kind of stupefied trance.

Auschwitz left me feeling beaten down by history, oppressed by a sense of its iron logic. The way it turned out was the way it had to turn out. No escape, no sidestepping ordained fate. Auschwitz was the last term of a mathematical proof.

But was that the only way to think about it? What would it have taken for Alexandre's story to have followed a narrative logic that didn't end at Auschwitz? Once more, as if I hadn't already worried the question endlessly, I asked myself just how much imagination or wisdom or whatever you want to call it would it have taken for Aronchik to see that things were falling apart and that it was time to leave France? I knew I was being unfair, disregarding the chaos of Aronchik's situation when it wasn't a matter of deciding between available choices but rather of seeing if choices even existed. In fact, getting out while the getting was good didn't depend only on understanding that the ground beneath your feet was crumbling. You had to be able to imagine more solid ground elsewhere. You had to imagine some other place to which to go.

America was the preferred option for many, but it wasn't the only one. Palestine was also a possible destination for endangered Jews. Zionist groups were active in almost every European country in the 1920s and 1930s, arguing the urgency of a return to the ancient homeland. Even some French Jews, who tended to be confident that their country would defend them against anti-Semitism, gave some thought to Palestine.

But there were also reasons to hesitate. Palestine's Arabs had by that time realized that Jews were intent on building a country, not just working a few farms, and had become unwelcoming. And the policy of the British Mandate authorities, despite the promises made in the Balfour Declaration, was strongly anti-immigration. They had enough on their hands managing the population that was already there.

I'm not sure how much either the Kahans or the Ripps knew about these political and social factors. Both knew something, that's for sure, but anyway that's not what was decisive in how they looked at Palestine as a possible home. What was most needed was a sense of personal connection. This was one of the points where the two families, the Kahans and the Ripps, took different paths, crucially. The Ripps had no personal connection with Palestine. The Kahans did. When the family left Berlin in 1933 and some thirty of them chose to go to Palestine, they were not leaping into the unknown. They were following a path laid down for them by previous generations.

Chaim Kahan, the patriarch of the family, was the son of a fishmonger who was also a melamed—someone who taught the Talmud to boys not suited to go to yeshiva. Doing a gritty, hands-on job during the week and interpreting the word of God on the Sabbath was not unusual for a Jew in a small Polish village in the mid-nineteenth century. Since there weren't enough rabbis to go around, other adults had to guide the children's spiritual development. His father's view of life as encompassing both the practical and the spiritual persisted in Chaim Kahan, though on a far grander scale.

A family memoir describes Chaim Kahan as a Jew in his tent and a man in the street. He celebrated the Sabbath, he kept kosher. He read the Talmud daily. Yiddish was his first language. But at the same time that he lived by Judaic law, he also engaged the outside world. He prospered in the tsarist oil industry when that was a battlefield of interests, worker sabotage on one side and owner cartels on the other. His business took him into offices of very wealthy Gentiles, where he more than held his own. It made sense that Chaim became attached to the Mizrachi, a group that advocated a commitment to both religion and practical affairs. One of the Mizrachi group's main efforts was helping Jews immigrate to Palestine. Chaim Kahan visited Palestine twice and donated large sums to the Yishuv.

Knowing Chaim Kahan's attachment to Palestine, on the occasion of his and his wife Malka's fiftieth wedding anniversary, his children got together and purchased a large tract of land in Palestine in his name. Mekor Chaim is now a residential neighborhood in the heart of Jerusalem. When the Kahans left Berlin for Palestine, they were going to a country where there was a plaque with the family patriarch's name on it. How much more personal an invitation did one need?

The family thrived in Palestine. Some became farmers—one of the land's largest orange groves, outside Tel Aviv, belonged to a Kahan. Another Kahan was a founder of Ma'agan Michael, still a working kibbutz today. The family helped to found the newspaper *Ha' aretz* and held significant shares in the chocolate maker Elite, a firm now listed on the Tel Aviv stock exchange. When I was growing up, there were often boxes of Elite chocolate in our New York apartment. At the time, taking large amounts of currency out of Israel was restricted, so though we owned Elite shares, we had no access to its profits. Sometimes it could seem that we were getting paid off in chocolate instead, though only a few pralines on the dollar.

It was my cousin Tani who made the biggest splash in Israeli life. There was a time when mentioning the name Tani Cohen-Mintz would be sure to make an Israeli smile in dreamy memory. Tani, who stood six foot eight, played center on the Maccabi basketball team when Israel was intent on showing the world that the country was populated by a new kind of Jew, one different from those who had too passively endured the Final Solution. When Tani led the Maccabi team to the final round of the European Cup of 1967, it was proof that the Sabra generation had arrived. When Tani died in 2014, newspapers ran obituaries on their front page. There was a public viewing of his casket.

The family in Israel eventually grew so numerous it became hard to remember every outlying third cousin or uncle twice removed. Here is an anecdote I liked to tell: Two teenagers played in the same weekly basketball game on a court in Tel Aviv. One Sunday, one of them said to the other, "I can't play next weekend, there's a family reunion I can't miss." The other said, "Really? Funny, I have a family reunion too." Sometimes I didn't even have to get to the punch line, my listeners were already smiling at the notion of family so big it was impossible to keep track of every relative.

But after I started on this project of tracing the history of the two families, repeating that anecdote made me uncomfortable, and I stopped. The mention of those weekly games, the offhand pleasures of guys getting together to run up and down the court and work up a good sweat, showed too vividly what Alexandre had missed. He was the boy who never had a chance to play basketball in Israel.

I wanted to see Grodno, the birthplace of my father and my uncle Aronchik. To get to Grodno from Kraków required crossing an international border. That's worth saying because over the years Grodno has pinballed among several countries, moved about by the caprices of war and politics—or, more exactly, Grodno stayed put but the borders around it kept getting redrawn. Imperial Russia, Lithuania, Germany, the Soviet Union, and Poland each had a turn at authority. In 2012, the name was changed to Hrodna, to mark the city as belonging to Belarus. That's how it stands at the moment, but history in these parts has left the impression that borders are temporary arrangements. Several locals told me they hoped to get Vilnius back from Lithuania and into Belarus where it belonged.

Belarus has had a special relationship with its northeastern neighbor. In 1919 parts of the country were absorbed by the Soviet Union as the Byelorussian Soviet Socialist Republic. Belarus became independent in 1991, but most natives speak Russian and not Belarusian. (The close relationship between the countries is reflected in English usage, which sometimes has the adjective "Belarussian" and sometimes "Belarusian.") Taking a stroll through Grodno's downtown, I came across a Red Army tank mounted on a pedestal in the central square. It was put there during the Cold War and pointed westward to symbolize Belarus's readiness to assist Russia should NATO attack. NATO's guns are silent, the tank remains.

Geopolitics also influences remembrance of the Holocaust here. It was only in 1991 that a memorial was placed at the head of the alleyway leading to where the ghetto was once located. That had to wait for the collapse of the Soviet Union. Till then there was an unstated policy that Jewish victims of the Nazis did not require particular commemoration. Millions of Soviet citizens died in the war, and Belarus was particularly hard-hit, with one in three citizens killed. Given such an enveloping catastrophe, why should the Jews get any special distinction? Yes, the Nazis had singled out Jews for destruction, but how much weight do the invaders' beliefs deserve? Though that view weakened after the Soviet Union collapsed, it did not disappear. The memorial at the ghetto entrance had to rely on funding from Belarusian Jews living abroad.

Having come to Belarus from Poland, I was aware of how tricky it could be to fit the Jewish tragedy into a country's view of its behavior in World War II. In both Poland and Belarus, actions by natives increased the number of victims that the Nazis managed to accumulate on their own. But there was a crucial distinction. Poles' killing of Jews was largely opportunistic. They took advantage of the chaos to enact long-standing anti-Semitic hatreds. Germany was always the prime enemy, there were few Polish collaborators. In Belarus there were many collaborators. The chance to kill Jews was an added benefit of taking the side of the Third Reich.

Shortly after arriving in Grodno, I went to have a look at the memorial on Zamkovaia Street, the site of one of Grodno's ghettos. It was in a residential neighborhood remote from the city center, and there were few passersby to take any notice. It makes sense to have a memorial here, at the site of Jewish victimization, but the out-of-the-way location has an unfortunate implication—that Grodno shies away from making too much of the tragedy

that overtook its Jews. There are several memorials that honor
Soviet citizens killed by the Germans. But this is the only Holocaust memorial in town.

There is a plaque in the alleyway that leads to where the ghetto
once was. A line of embossed figures stretches toward the background of the plaque. They gradually get smaller, and finally fade
away into the bronze. The absence of a clear end point to the line
of figures mirrors the condition of Jews during the Holocaust—
disappearing in numbers beyond counting.

The figures are well dressed, some of the men in suits and ties.
The man in front carries what looks like a suitcase or perhaps a
large briefcase. Another figure, a bald head cut off just below eye
level by the representation of a wall, seems to be looking out from
within a confined space. That establishes the marchers' destination. They are headed for a ghetto. These are Jews before the worst
overtakes them.

Facts about the German occupation of Grodno are easily
available on the Internet. There were two ghettos. Ghetto B in the
suburb of Slobodka was for those too old or infirm to work. Ghetto
A, which was entered from the alleyway on Zamkovaia Street,
was for the healthy. The two ghettos came into existence in
November 1941. I'm fairly sure my relatives were confined in
Ghetto A.

The Judenrat, composed of ten community leaders, adminis-
tered daily life in Ghetto A. Hot meals were served daily, free to
those who could not afford to pay. A plot was set aside to grow
vegetables. A makeshift economy came into being, with shops that
sold goods smuggled from outside or that were produced in workshops in the ghetto. Shoes, sheet metal, clothes, and other neces-
sities were available, if only sporadically and in minute quantity.

The Internet gave me facts, but not what I wanted to know
most: How did my relatives get through each day? How did they

manage the wrench from a life of comfortable habits to one of constant uncertainty? What new attitudes had to be cultivated, what values and beliefs had to be altered or abandoned? There is a memoir by a survivor of Ghetto A, and I thought it might provide an answer to these questions.

Felix Zandman was thirteen years old when he and his family were ordered into the ghetto. He was aware that food was scarce and that people were beaten and tormented. There were rumors of killings. But routines were soon established, and Zandman was able to write, "To me, life seemed more or less normal. Or maybe I was just getting used to the conditions."*

Connections with the world outside the ghetto still existed, and Zandman took advantage. With several friends he bought tobacco on the black market and packaged it with labels that looked as if they came from Grodno's large tobacco factory. The father of a friend had a shop within the ghetto and agreed to sell the tobacco. As Zandman puts it, "We were in business."

The young people in the ghetto spent most of their time together. Freed from strict parental supervision, they smoked cigarettes and flirted and found sexual pleasure. Zandman writes, "There was kissing and touching behind closed doors and in alleys, just as I suppose we would have done had there been no ghetto." Zandman was proficient with the violin, and he joined a chamber music quartet. He writes, "If life continued like this I could live this way for a hundred years."

But it didn't continue that way. One day, German soldiers broke into the room occupied by the Zandman family and ransacked it. Finding Zandman's violin, a Gestapo officer plucked its strings, put it under his chin, and began to play. Zandman notes, "It wasn't bad, I thought, he obviously had some train-

*Felix Zandman. *Never the Last Journey*, 44ff.

ing." But then the officer stopped playing, took the violin by the neck, and smashed it against the wall. Germans might appear civilized, but the death's-head was right beneath the skin.

Beatings now occurred daily. Shootings became more common. Zandman's chamber music quartet one day abruptly became a trio. The randomness of fate was embodied by the ghetto commandant, Kurt Wiese, who always dressed in a black uniform with shiny silver zippers and buttons. The Jews called him Malach ha-Mavet, the Angel of Death. He had the habit of shooting into crowds when the mood took him.

At one point Zandman found himself in a position to kill Wiese—an ax was at hand, Wiese was unsuspecting. But Zandman let the opportunity pass. The encounter shows a young man driven to the limits of his civilized nature, and it also reminded me what I was reading. The violin playing, the flirtations, the tobacco scam, as well as the urge to kill—this was the experience of one man. Call his story "Life in the ghetto: the moral education of a young Jew." But because Zandman tells such a personal story, the experience of the Ripps gets illuminated only dimly. Events after the ghetto was evacuated underscore the differences. Zandman's story is of a triumph against the odds. He escaped the Nazis' grasp, eventually immigrated to America, and invented a technological device that became the basis of a Fortune 500 company. The Ripps' story is a mute tragedy. There is no chronicle of their murder. I know they died in one of the camps, but I'm not sure which.

I have some idea of how the Ripps lived in Grodno at the turn of the twentieth century, in those years long before the Nazis arrived and destroyed the Jewish community. My knowledge comes from family table talk and from a few official documents that I managed to get hold of. There was also a taped interview with Sula, the younger sister of Aronchik and my father. She left Grodno when still young, so her memories of that city were cloudy and brief—picnics by the Neman River, excitement when the Jewish theater group Habima came to town, not much more. But her final comment, and the tone in which she said it, left an impression. "Life was good there," she said, switching from a bland declarative to a dreamy cadence.

Sula's father (Alexandre's and my grandfather) was Leima Ripp—Lev, to friends and family. He came to Grodno toward the end of the nineteenth century, from Nesvizh, a town south of Minsk. Nesvizh was the home of the Radziwills, one of Belarus's most illustrious families. At one point the Radziwills owned all of the land the town was situated on, and their palace and grounds dominated the town. The palace had a moat, which symbolizes Nesvizh's two-part social structure—one family enjoying great wealth, and the rest of the population, Lev's family included, eking out an existence.

Soon after Lev came of age, he left Nesvizh. He was looking for better economic opportunities but also wanted to escape the religious observances imposed by his father, who was zealous in his beliefs. In reaction, Lev became strongly antireligious. I have seen the birth certificate of his eldest son—my father—where the name is entered as Solomon Ripp. Solomon, not Shlomo. That Russification of a name was a symbolic rejection of traditional Judaism.

Lev's move away from orthodoxy was part of a trend. For many years, a Jew's life in Russia had been supervised by the *kahal*, the council of elders in each Jewish community. Jews paid their taxes to the kahal and in return the kahal provided education, support for the indigent, and health care. The kahal stood between the individual Jew and the often antagonistic tsarist bureaucracy, and for that a Jew was grateful. The price for that protection was conformity to strict religious norms.

But beginning in mid-century, and increasingly in the years when Lev came to adulthood, the kahal lost its influence as many Jews stood ready to engage Russian society. They favored Russian over Yiddish, attended government-run schools instead of chedars and yeshivas, moved from shtetls to towns and cities. The kahal was associated with obscurantism and, often, corruption, making it appear all the more an institution whose day had passed. Assimilation into the larger society was never an unambiguous step, and indeed many Jews advocated positions short of that extreme. But, all in all, looking around, Lev could see a Russian Jewry that was becoming transformed.

That transformation was limited and monitored by the tsarist regime. Beginning in the late eighteenth century, when Russia acquired millions of Jews consequent to its annexation of Polish territory, government policy restricted Jews in a variety of ways, including confinement to a Pale of Settlement. But the government was also wary of allowing Jews to remain a group apart, fearing the creation of a nation within a nation. In periodic efforts to resolve the paradox, the government permitted some controlled integration. Reforms in the mid- and late nineteenth century eased Jewish entry into the judiciary, expanded commercial opportunities, and—most dramatically—gave Jewish university graduates unrestricted residence rights. But full rights of citizenship were still denied, and the government did nothing to halt the periodic pogroms.

When Lev moved to Grodno, he found a city where Jewish life was flourishing. Jews were fifty percent of the population and most of the shops were owned by Jews. The two largest employers in the city—a tobacco factory and a motorcycle factory—were owned by Jews, as were several of the banks. Even the fire brigade was Jewish.

Lev married Eva Frank, the daughter of the owner of a dry

goods shop. Flour, blankets, pots and pans—that's the sort of thing I imagined were for sale. Owning a shop was a typical occupation for Jews in the tsarist era, when they were barred from many ways of making a living. Most struggled to make ends meet. You didn't get rich as a shopkeeper. Regarding Lev's particular case, I could only speculate. Having gone as far as I could with the material I had at hand, I was eager for some on-the-ground investigation.

A friend who had recently passed through Grodno had recommended I get in touch with Tatiana Kasataia. She was a passionate local historian, adept at archival work. I knew from a year doing academic research in what was then Leningrad that the tsarist bureaucracy tried to get every aspect of Russian life down on paper. Who lived where, the taxes they paid, their occupation, the number of children, and so on. But once that information was deposited in the archives, it became almost impossible to track down. The records of those past lives transubstantiated into elusive ghosts. Chaos reigned in the library stacks, the staff shrugged off pleas for help. But Tatiana had dug deep and come up with the goods.

On the first day we met, she brought me to a quiet residential street near the main synagogue. "This is the house where your grandmother and grandfather—Leima and Eva Ripp—lived from 1900 to 1914. Thirty-two Zamkovaia Street. Down the street from where the ghetto used to be. See that big house next to theirs?" She pointed.

It was more mansion than house. Two large wings off the main central section, a prepossessing courtyard. Tatiana said, "It belonged to Shereshevsky, the owner of the tobacco factory. He was probably the richest man in Grodno."

I was taken aback that my grandfather could afford such a classy neighborhood. But that wasn't the only surprise. I had assumed he was an outsider, a newcomer with no easy entry into Grodno society. But Tatiana had found documents showing that Leima Ripp had become very much an insider. He was a member of the Society for the Support of Jewish Students, cochairman of the Council for Support for the Care of Jewish Orphans, a member of the Zionist club Palestine.

Tatiana said, "When the kahal stopped doing as much, private associations took up the slack. It wasn't unusual for a Jew of a certain class to join several of them."

The spot where the Franks' store had been located was within walking distance, and we set off. Sovetskaia Street was a heavily trafficked pedestrian mall, and according to Tatiana it was as popular when it was called Sobornaia Street and the Franks' store was open for business. The city's main marketplace had been at one end of the street, filled with the stalls of farmers and craftsmen. People who came to stock up on vegetables or horseshoes or farming tools often spilled over onto Sobornaia, looking for more things to buy.

Tatiana pointed to the building in the middle of the block, which had once housed the Franks' business. It was not the cramped and shoddy shop of my imagination but an elegant two-story structure. The store had been at street level, with the living quarters one flight up. Tatiana's research had turned up evidence that the business had prospered. It mainly sold expensive imported fabrics at a time when most people made their own clothes.

I was several times amazed by what Tatiana found in the archives, and now she did it again. She had come across documents showing that there had been two cinemas on Sobornaia Street right near the Franks' store—the Electro-Biograf and the Lux.

Joking, I told Tatiana that she could probably even tell me what was on the bill back when Lev and Eva were likely to have gone to the movies.

"Give me a few hours, I'll get back to you," she said.

Later that day Tatiana sent me an e-mail. "Here are some of the movies that were in theaters when your grandfather and grandmother lived in Grodno: *Fal'shivii kupon* (The Forged Coupon), *Zhizn' evreev v Palestine* (The Life of Jews in Palestine), *Pod vlastiu strasti* (Under the Spell of Passion), *Noch' v buduare* (Night in the Boudoir).

I tried to decipher the titles, treating them as coded messages from a Grodno as it was a century ago. *The Forged Coupon* was based on a Tolstoy novella that depicts every institution of Russian society, from the family to the church, as hypocritical. Sitting in the darkened theater, Grodno's Jews surely would have nodded in agreement. The film about Palestine was a dream of paradise that must have seemed more compelling with each report of a pogrom somewhere in Russia. The titles *Under the Spell of Passion* and *Night in the Boudoir* were tantalizing. Maybe watching the films stirred curiosity about love in the rest of the world. What, I wondered, if my grandparents Lev and Eva had seen these films? How did they feel about the extravagant goings-on depicted on the screen? I was playing at detective, reading clues, making inferences.

Toward evening, Tatiana called and suggested a walk on the other side of the Neman before it got too dark. We crossed over a stone bridge and passed through a quiet park, then stopped at the Church of Saints Boris and Gleb, a small jewel of twelfth-century architecture. Tatiana pointed to the tinted stones worked into the façade, noting that they could be found only in this region. Farther on, there was a spectacular view of Noviy Zamek (New Palace), the residence of Polish kings in the seventeenth century, one of the intervals when Polish kings had a country to rule. On the riverbank, a lone fisherman was trying his luck.

This was the spot, I felt sure, of my aunt Sula's fondly remembered picnics. The stretch of lawn was nondescript, in no way special, but I felt it had an aura of happiness and good times. Of course I was too ready to endow the spot with significance. I wanted to believe there was a moment when the Ripps had enjoyed life before their world turned bleak.

An evening chill had come on, and I put on my cap, remarking to Tatiana that in America it was believed that eighty percent of body heat escapes via the head.

"Here we believe it escapes through the feet, which is why in winter everyone wears really heavy socks," Tatiana said, thus defining the distance that lay between me and an understanding of my ancestral home.

There was another memorial in Grodno I wanted to see. It was less a Holocaust memorial than an anti-Holocaust memorial. In 1950, with the ravages of the Nazis still a living memory, preserving every vestige of Jewish culture should have been an obvious obligation. That was the moment the Soviet authorities decided to erect a sports stadium on the grounds of Grodno's old Jewish cemetery. The official justification was that getting life back to normal outweighed any sentimental remembrance. But the manner of the construction suggested something nastier. Some gravestones were uprooted and used to pave roads.

In 2003, during repairs on a part of the stadium, some human remains were unearthed. There were rumors that sand from the work site, which overlay the old cemetery, was being used to fill sandpits in the city playgrounds. The public outcry was loud enough for the authorities to set a commemorative plaque just outside the stadium, though it was so modest that I almost missed it when I went looking for it. The writing was in Hebrew and Belarusian. Translated, it reads "In memory of those Jews who from the fourteenth century lived on the land of Grodno." There is no reference to a Jewish cemetery, no hint of remorse. The inscription, vague and banal, seemed to me only to repeat the willed ignorance it should have been apologizing for.

But I was glad to have seen this memorial. It was worthwhile to be reminded that the Holocaust was only the most extreme instance of anti-Semitism in these parts. Nazis sowed their atrocities on well-prepared land. Jews in tsarist Russia were oppressed in various ways, and their life was no better in Soviet Russia. And then there were the Poles. My father's stories about his life in Grodno when it was under Polish authority were vague. He seemed to circle around key moments, which was unlike him. He was an optimist, always energetic, never letting bad luck keep him down. My guess is that his Grodno stories were vague because for once he had been unable to find his way around obstacles. When I knew I was going to visit Grodno, I had tried to fill in the gaps in his stories with some research.

For all that I read, a single historical fact seemed to me to sum up the circumstances of my father's time in Polish-controlled Grodno. To secure its status as an independent country after World War I, Poland had to sign the Minorities Treaty. This was sometimes called the Little Treaty of Versailles, which suggests an innocuous afterthought to serious matters, though in fact it was formulated to meet a dire threat. Minorities, and especially Jews, had long been mistreated in the territories designated to become Poland, and the war and its chaotic aftermath had made their situation even more precarious. The treaty required the Polish government to guarantee minorities access to public employment, educational opportunities, and civic and political rights. Apparently, Poles were so eager to deny minorities their rights that only an international treaty could restrain them.

Tatiana suggested that I speak to Boris Kviatovsky. His

father had lived through that period, 1921 forward, and he had anecdotes about how it was back then.

I met Boris in a small anteroom of Grodno's Great Synagogue. He was the head of Grodno's Jewish community, a position that made him a commander with virtually no troops. He told me that usually only two or three worshippers showed up for Saturday services. Though lacking a minyan, the services went forward anyway, which didn't surprise me. It was of a piece with the catch-as-catch-can mood that prevailed in the synagogue when I was there. The main hall was being restored and was a shambles. In the interval, services were held in the small anteroom, which was filled with a jumble of tables and folding chairs. Carpenters, painters, and office workers circulated without obvious purpose or result.

Boris led me into an adjoining room that served as a makeshift museum. There were some random religious items in two vitrines, but what caught my eye were the photographs of famous Grodno Jews hanging on a wall. I studied one in particular.

Boris spoke up. "Meyer Lansky, he was born in Grodno. He gave a lot of money to Israel. He deserves a place in our museum no matter what else he did."

What else he did, of course, was to form a major crime syndicate with Lucky Luciano and Bugsy Siegel. It got him extradited from Israel, where he had fled in hopes of avoiding U.S. prosecution.

I asked why there was no photo of Léon Bakst, who was also a native of Grodno. Bakst designed sets and costumes for Diaghilev's Ballets Russes, and he was of special interest to me because his spectacularly multicolored print of Sadko, a figure in Russian folklore, hung in the living room of my family's apartment when I was growing up. My mother bought it shortly after we arrived in America, paying only a couple of dollars to a used-furniture dealer on Columbus Avenue who didn't know what he was selling. That was lucky, since though she was eager to give the print as a gift to my father to remind him of his hometown, she couldn't have afforded what it was really worth. Now it hangs in my living room, my only tangible connection to Grodno.

Boris said, "Bakst? He was Leyb Rosenberg when he lived in Grodno, but he forgot he was Jewish when he became famous. So we forgot him." His tone was matter-of-fact, a simple assertion of local pride, but I felt I had been moved a little further away from my heritage.

Boris led me back into the anteroom, pulled out two folding chairs for us to sit on, and began to talk more or less nonstop. "At first, in 1921, when the Poles took over, it wasn't so bad. No one interfered with Jewish political activities. There were Zionist groups, Bundists, Revisionists, and each of these had a social hall. One had its own orchestra. There was even a Jewish football team. All of Grodno celebrated when it defeated some other city in a match. Whether there were good relations because everyone was feeling happy because of the new independence or because of the Minorities Treaty, I can't say.

"It got bad soon enough. More and more Poles moved in. They were attracted by government subsidies to buy land. Soon, if you weren't Polish, you couldn't work in a government position. The law was that Jews could attend schools, but that didn't mean they were welcome. They were made to stand in the back of the hall for all the lectures, bullies intentionally bumped into them in the hallways, looking for an excuse for a fight. And it got even worse. Boycotts of Jewish stores, closing down of Jewish neighborhood social centers. For a Jew to walk through the Polish section of town at night was very risky. At the least he would be beaten."

I knew my father had been harassed by Polish thugs, but had he actually been beaten? I didn't trust Boris's self-certain style, which offhandedly turned possibility into fact, but something bad could have occurred. My father would not have accepted restrictions on where he could walk in his hometown.

He left Grodno for Germany in the 1920s, though I'm not sure of the exact date. In Berlin, he enrolled in the Handels Hochschule, a graduate school of business. His diploma, which I have, indicates that upon finishing his studies, "Solomon Ripp aus Grodno" received the grade of "gut" from the school's auditing commission. He was on his way to a new life. Any humiliation he had endured in Grodno, whether or not it included a beating, seems to have served only to propel him forward.

I have filled in some gaps in the story of my father's life, going beyond what he told me. The pieces seem to fit, and there is a satisfaction in that. But at the same time, I'm somewhat uneasy. Is it right for me to compose an account of my father's life that he didn't want to compose himself? I mean, he was my father, not a character in a short story.

Rosh Hashanah fell on a day when I was in Grodno, and I decided to go to services. Given what I had seen of the synagogue, I didn't expect much. I was going mainly out of sociological curiosity. Boris had said that the Jews who had come to Grodno after World War II were very different from those who had lived in Grodno when my relatives were there.

"Homo Sovieticus," Boris called them. "Engineers, scientists, managers, none of them interested in religion. You need God when there is no other option, which is how it was back then. These new Jews had options, or thought they did. That's the kind we have now in Grodno. The Soviet Union may be gone, but Homo Sovieticus lives on."

His comment served to organize some random thoughts that

had been running through my mind the last few days. Grodno's story, I decided, was not a continuous rolling out of events, where each new stage developed organically from the one that came immediately before. There were, rather, successive traumatic moments when the city was jolted into overhauling its nature completely. Grodno's past consisted of discrete segments, one laid atop the other. The best way to look at Grodno's past was not as history but as archaeology.

The scheduled service on the first night of Rosh Hashanah was canceled. Most of Belarus was served by one rabbi, and he was busy in Minsk. The next day, however, it was SRO. Some fifty people crowded into the small anteroom. The Jewish community in Grodno may have hibernated during most of the year, but the High Holy Days got them out and about.

The service was over in record time, twenty minutes tops. Homo Sovieticus apparently required no extended religious balm. Speaking heavily accented Russian, the rabbi—from Chicago, it turned out—delivered a homily on the inherent goodness of misbehaving students. The congregation joined in a few songs, reading off sheets of transliterated lyrics. An attack on the table of food followed. It all seemed slapdash, formulaic. Rosh Hashanah for the brave new world.

As we milled about on the street outside the synagogue, the rabbi said a few more words before inviting the congregation to walk with him to the Neman. "The Bible tells us that on this day we should go and throw our sins into the sea. Grodno has no sea. So the river will have to do."

Twenty or so of us started walking toward the Neman through the indifferent city streets with the rabbi in the lead. After about ten minutes, our procession halted at a high embankment that gave out on a spectacular view of the river. We were a motley group—parents rocking prams with crying babies, teenagers whispering their lives into mobile devices, a couple of guys staring out into space thinking deep thoughts or no thoughts at all. But when the rabbi blew the shofar, everyone snapped to rapt attention. The lambent air suddenly seemed to fill with meaning.

Afterwards there was handshaking all around. Several people approached me, welcoming the visitor from America and anxiously asking if anyone there had ever heard of Grodno. I was the proxy prodigal son, standing in for my father and uncle who had left almost a century ago.

I should be clear. I didn't have a transcendent spiritual experience, a moment when the trappings of this world fell away. As a secular Jew, I don't respond that way to religious ritual. But I did have an unexpected insight, one that seemed to bring the past closer. I felt more fully attuned to the life of the Ripps in Grodno than I had been before. The intervening years no longer felt like a blockage; they felt like a series of events stretching from there to here. And I felt I belonged to the latest stage of that history, even if only awkwardly.

That moment by the Neman didn't include a memorial, but it did suggest something about remembrance that, I decided, might apply to memorials as well. The stars have to be in alignment, all the elements have to be in place, if a memorial is to be effective—and one of those elements is the viewer. You have to find your proper place in the particular stretch of history that the memorial invokes. Tenuously connected or deeply involved, it doesn't matter which, as long as you are honest.

My father and his brother Aronchik were very close, and for a while they traveled pretty much in tandem, first to Germany and then to France. But my father got his family—my mother, brother, and me—out of harm's way while much of Aronchik's family was swallowed up by the Nazi killing machine. The different destinies can't be explained by one or two decisions. But there was a moment when the paths of the brothers began to diverge. That happened when my father married into the Kahan family. Though he was never fully accepted, being the son of a dry goods merchant, his choices and actions became tied up with those of the Kahans. And the Kahans were the ones who escaped the Final Solution.

When I think of the Kahan family history, I think of my maternal grandmother, born Zina Golodetz in the shtetl of Shchedrin. There was a Holocaust memorial there in a defunct Jewish cemetery, and that was a reason to go. But I also wanted to see Zina's birthplace.

Zina married Pinchas Kahan in 1900. The wedding took place in Baranovichi, a railroad hub eight miles from Shchedrin. There's a photo of the wedding party posing at the railroad station, looking as if they've missed their train and are resigned to a long wait for the next one. The odd location for a wedding made sense. The wedding merged two wealthy families, each proud of its pedigree, and Baranovichi served as neutral ground. Pinchas, one of five sons of Chaim Kahan, ran that part of the family oil business that operated out of Baku. The Golodetzes were as well off as the Kahans, deriving their wealth from their lumber business. It certainly wasn't a love match. The bride and groom had met only twice before and then only briefly, to size each other up. The first meeting had not gone well. Neither party was enthusiastic. The second meeting went well enough for matters to move forward.

The marriage may have begun inauspiciously, but it proved happy for as long as it lasted. It ended when Pinchas died of a heart attack in 1917 at the age of forty-six. Zina didn't retreat into muted widowhood. Rather, she stepped up her participation in the family business. After Chaim Kahan's death in 1916, his seven children had inherited equal voting rights. Zina held Pinchas's vote, and since there were often disputes about the operation of the business, her role was crucial. But her influence went beyond a single vote. She was short, a bit more than five feet, not particularly beautiful, but it was not her appearance that made others defer to her. I think it was that her manner suggested that she expected deference, and she played that role so convincingly that others fell in with her view of herself.

By the time Zina taped her recollections of growing up in Shchedrin, she was in her nineties and would die within two years. Her commentary is discontinuous, the narrative line jumpy. But she gets the main points across. Listening to the tape gave me a picture of the town. On the one hand, it was so unworldly that Zina saw an electric light for the first time on her honeymoon, in a Kharkov hotel room. She spent hours switching the lights on and off, marveling at the miracle. But growing up in Shchedrin also endowed Zina with a steely self-confidence that would prove useful in 1930s Europe.

I've heard several versions of how Shchedrin was founded. One was by a native who left for good as a teenager in 1917 and spent his adult life in Soviet Russia. His description is of a piece with Soviet communism's effort to blacken every aspect of tsarist Russia. Jews were portrayed as one more group that was defenseless against the whims of a cruel and exploitative regime.

In 1840, so this story goes, Tsar Nicholas I toured the region to inspect battlements and troop dispositions. Jews, afraid that the officers of the party would enforce a Russian version of droit du seigneur, shaved the heads of their daughters and otherwise deprettified them. Nevertheless, one officer stepped away from the tsar's retinue and demanded the name and address of one young girl who stood by the road watching the passing parade. The officer declared he would make his visit to her that night. But before the appointed hour, the whole family decamped from

town, and looking for safety they settled in what became Shchedrin. That might have been how it happened, certainly tsarist
officers were no angels. But I tend to doubt it. The story fits too
neatly with the Communist party line.

The second version, in a memoir by a descendant of the found-
ers, is more persuasive. According to existing law, any Jew who
settled at least one hundred Jews on land outside the cities was
awarded the rank of honorary citizen, which brought with it certain privileges, including exemption from military service for all
members of the family. Sometime in the 1840s, the Lubavitcher
Rabbi Menachem Mendel Schneerson bought four hundred acres
in Minsk gubernia. The Golodetzes purchased one hundred of
these. The rest of the land was given rent-free to Jews of lesser
means. It's worth noting that today's Lubavitchers contend Schneerson was motivated by generosity toward his coreligionists and not
a desire for rank. But the result, a Jewish community on previously uninhabited land, would have been the same in both cases.

The community included blacksmiths, teachers, and various
craftsmen. Farming, which at first had seemed might pay off,
failed to take hold because the terrain was made swampy by the
recurrent flooding of the Berezina River. The Golodetzes were
the biggest employer by far. The only non-Jews were a few families
at the edge of town and the *Shabbos goy* who kept the town
running by doing those things Jews were forbidden from doing
on the Sabbath. By 1881, when my grandmother was born, Shchedrin had three thousand inhabitants.

The extended Golodetz family, numbering about one hundred,
lived on a small hill at the edge of town, in a fifteen-house complex formed around a courtyard. There was a town council, but
only members of the Golodetz family served on it. The Golodetzes had their own shul and sent their children to their own
schools. On those occasions when they went to the town shul,

they sat in the privileged seats near the eastern wall. The town and the family shared the single doctor and the ritual butcher, and on market days everyone intermingled freely. But those few democratic gestures didn't disguise the town's hierarchy.

Zina said, "Everyone understood who was who—who was a blacksmith, who was upper class. Who had a cart, who had a carriage. When we passed by, townspeople would say, that's the ones from the courtyard."

Zina was unapologetic about her family's prosperity. "Every summer we went abroad, usually to the Baltic, to Germany. One year we went to Marienbad for four weeks to take the waters, then to some other resort for two weeks to rest from taking the waters." That suggests the arrogance of wealth. But there's a more admirable aspect also. It's the voice of someone who moved through the world with ease at a time when Jews were constrained to stay where they had been put. It was a good quality to have when the Nazis came to power.

Shchedrin's daily life was shot through with anxieties and prejudices. But these feelings had a special flavor. Zina told an anecdote about the strategy she followed when visiting a friend after dark. "When I left and headed for home," she said, "I would keep shouting, 'I am walking, I am walking.' This was to assure my friend I had not been attacked and was still alive." But, Zina noted, what she and her friend feared were witches and golems and not a Cossack pogrom. For Shchedrin's Jewish inhabitants, the main concern of the day was attending to the rules and habits of their own culture, not worrying about attacks from the world beyond the shtetl.

Shchedrin's self-confidence followed from its economic power. The influence of a typical shtetl extended only as far as the immediately surrounding peasantry, for whom it provided two services—vodka and an inn in which to drink it, and assistance in bringing farm produce to market. No one in a typical shtetl was very rich. But the Golodetzes had developed their lumber business into an enterprise whose influence extended to distant points of Russia, and they were very rich.

Some of their methods were innovative, transforming Russia's lumber industry. In the winter, the forests were cleared by peasants and the logs hauled by sled to a nearby stream. When the ice melted, rafts of about two hundred logs each were towed to the Dnieper, then floated to market towns downriver. Each "lot" required some thirty workers, who had to be housed and fed.

In 1882, thanks to the Golodetzes' commercial success, the head of the family received the title of hereditary honorary citizen. It was certified with a document that listed all members of the Golodetz family and was affixed with the seal of the tsarist Senate. No wonder Golodetzes had confidence, dealing with Russians on an equal footing as few Jews could.

One spectacular instance of the Golodetzes' readiness to engage the outside world was the purchase of Lialichi, the country estate built by Catherine the Great for her lover Count Pyotr Zavadovsky. It was designed by Bartolomeo Rastrelli, who also designed sections of the Winter Palace in Saint Petersburg. The three-story structure had 120 rooms, including a bedroom for Catherine. The story, usually accompanied by knowing smiles, was that she once spent three nights there.

When the Golodetzes acquired Lialichi, its glory days were over. The roof leaked, the plumbing was corroded. But the house was still sumptuously appointed with many valuable items—which the Golodetzes immediately sold off. Oak parquet floors, Turkish rugs, mahogany furniture, gold bathroom fixtures—all went to auction. It was scandalous that this jewel of eighteenth-century Russian design should be dismantled piece by piece, but even more shocking was that Jews could outbid Russians for the property.

Purchasing Lialichi was part of the Golodetzes' shrewd business vision. They had their eye on the one thousand surrounding acres that were included in the sale. That expanse included forests that could be harvested for lumber.

According to Zina, "The Golodetz family was not interested in Russian culture. Buying Lialichi was to make a profit."

She didn't mean this as criticism. The Golodetzes' success in business in a Christian world was something to be proud of. It was a lesson that she didn't forget when she left Shchedrin: Be confident and the world will prove to be more assailable than it might appear.

Shchedrin was a three-hour drive from Minsk. On the way, the driver I hired kept chattering about America's misbehavior in neighboring Ukraine. Laughing, Misha told me that a White House spokesperson had said America was considering sending the Sixth Fleet to patrol Belarus's coastline. Belarus is, of course, landlocked. It was amusing the first time I heard the anecdote, but this was the third rendition since my arrival.

Passing through Bobruisk, we stopped to pick up Faina Mendeleev. Her mother had lived in Shchedrin in the interwar period, and Faina would provide some guidance based on what she had heard around the family dinner table. But as we drove along, Faina never mentioned Shchedrin. Instead, she talked nonstop about how life had changed for the worse since the collapse of the Soviet Union. Why was it so hard to get the death certificate of her father who had died defending the Fatherland against the Fascists? Why were today's bureaucrats so impolite? Civic life used to present a human face, but no more. In her telling, the Brezhnev era was one of humanity's golden ages.

I began to feel that the purpose of this trip was getting lost.

Between Misha's commentary on the current crisis in Ukraine and Faina's nostalgia for the Soviet Union, my interest in my grandmother's shtetl seemed to recede into the irrelevant past. But once we drove into Shchedrin, the purpose of my trip came back into focus. Looking around, it wasn't hard to imagine we were back in the nineteenth century.

The town was one main street with several smaller streets, paths really, running off of it. Stray dogs patrolled the alleys, groups of old men sat on the stoops. The only action on view was a makeshift roadside market consisting of a couple of tables. Small, shriveled apples and old clothes were for sale, though no one was buying. A few of the houses were painted gaudy blue, which only emphasized the general dreariness.

I had considered taking a bus to Shchedrin, and I now saw that would have been disastrous. The cemetery was two miles out of town, and getting around on my own would have been impossible. The town was not set up to accommodate the incidental traveler. There were no public buses, no taxis, though maybe I could have found a horse and cart for hire.

I was eager to get to the cemetery and the Holocaust memorial that was there, but Faina insisted we first have a look at the memorial to the local Hero of the Soviet Union, who had gotten his award for actions during the Great Patriotic War against Germany. I reluctantly complied. The memorial was about ten minutes' walk followed by time allotted to photographing. I have a photo of me posed with Faina in front of a statuette and facsimile of a medal. I look annoyed, and no wonder—this was a detour from the task at hand, another instance of the logjam of events that blocked a clear view of the family history that I was interested in.

The cemetery was located in a hilly area safe from the recurrent flooding of the nearby Berezina River. We navigated switchback dirt roads that tested Misha's driving skills. At various points the shoulder by the side of the road disappeared, at other points there was neither road nor shoulder. We rounded a sharp curve and came to an abrupt stop. One minute I had been thinking only about what medical treatment was available in Shchedrin for car crash victims, the next minute we were at our destination.

The plot was divided into two. To the left, a sign marked the old Jewish cemetery, dating to the nineteenth century. Think of an American cemetery, everything neatly in place, laid out according to a rational plan. This was the opposite. The gravestones, which lay flat on the ground, were set at random. Green moss covered their surfaces, rendering the inscriptions illegible. The terrain, marked by stumpy trees and uncovered roots, made walking difficult, and in general the cemetery appeared to barely resist the encroaching vegetation. But if the cemetery seemed on the edge of oblivion, what nevertheless most struck me was that against all odds it was still holding on. I was wary of attributing significance to what after all was only an accident of nature, but I couldn't resist: what I saw before me seemed proof of the persistence of the spirit of Judaism, its will to survive.

Near the middle of the other part of the plot there was a stone pillar about fifteen feet high. It was pockmarked but not otherwise damaged. The inscription included the usual reference to "peace-loving victims of Nazi aggression" without noting that the victims were Jews, and the Soviet star on the top of the memorial was one more insistence that the Jewish tragedy had to be folded into the larger national one. But the abutting old Jewish cemetery was an argument against that governmental dictum, its existence an assertion that the spirit of Judaism persisted in Shchedrin even in the worst of times. The two parts of the cemetery were of a piece, it seemed to me, equally sacred Jewish land.

A stretch of raised earth ran alongside the pillar and then faded out in the middle distance. Faina told me that some five hundred Jews were buried here. Because no clear markings divided the mass grave from the surrounding terrain, from one angle it could appear that the mound extended to infinity. It was as if death had no limit, that there was no reason for the killing ever to have stopped.

Some Holocaust memorials in Belarus have been vandalized, some destroyed. It would have been nice to believe there was a logic that explained why the one in Shchedrin remains untouched. Maybe towns, like people, have memories. Maybe Shchedrin has retained enough of its original self-confident Jewishness to somehow ward off any attack on the memorial. That version of events, with its theme of enduring Jewish power, was appealing, but of course towns have memories only in legends. In the real world what likely happened was that with no Jews left in Shchedrin to persecute, anti-Semitism went into remission. And the Holocaust memorial came to seem just an unremarkable part of the landscape, nothing worth bothering about. It was like that old philosophical saw. If a tree falls in the forest and no one is around to hear it, does it still make a sound? If no one notices a Holocaust memorial, does it still have significance?

On the road back to Bobruisk, Faina abruptly told Misha to pull over. I couldn't see the point. We were in a desolate landscape, with no sign of any human enterprise even to the far horizon. But once we drove farther along on an off-path, we came to a parking lot large enough to accommodate a hundred cars, though empty now. There were signs posting the hours of operation, where to dispose of trash, other rules of conduct. Clearly we were at some sort of tourist destination, though it was hard to imagine what points of interest might be found in this godforsaken spot. Another sign dispelled the mystery. We were at the site of a Holocaust memorial, though of a very particular kind.

The memorial honors Jewish children who were forced to donate their blood to wounded German soldiers, a postponement but not a reprieve from the gas chambers. This procedure threatened to contaminate the soldiers' Aryan stock, but wartime needs took precedence. Care was taken, however, that the soldiers never knew the source of their transfusions. A large map marked the location of several camps in Belarus where the macabre procedure took place.

Thank God, I told myself. Alexandre was at least spared this barbarity.

The memorial extends over an area of some sixty feet, and consists of two distinct elements. In the first, ten rows of concrete benches are arranged to resemble student desks in a classroom. The benches are painted white, emphasizing their ghostliness. No students will return to take up their studies. Young lives have been ended before their natural term.

The second element strikes a very different note, dogmatic where the benches are suggestive. Displayed on a flat upright surface is an enlarged facsimile of a letter written by a fifteen-year-old girl to her father. Of course it is phony—the Germans hardly allowed prisoners to write letters home, as if from summer camp. "Dear Papa, when you read this I will be dead. Mother is already dead. But I am sure we will be avenged, that the Fascist invader will be defeated," and so on in the hyperpatriotic style of Communist Young Pioneer groups. Sentimentality lurks in the wings of many Holocaust memorials—here it steps onto the stage for a full-throated aria. The false feeling of the letter seeped over the rest of the memorial. Now I couldn't look at those white desks without imagining them filled with Young Pioneers, all professing their allegiance to Mother Russia.

As we got back into the car, Faina said, "It's not the right time of year. This parking lot is often full. Schoolchildren on excursions mainly. They have to learn about the Holocaust."

Of course, what they would learn in this case was that the Holocaust was a subdivision of Soviet Russia's Great Patriotic War. That the Germans were monsters and the spirit of the Soviet people was indomitable. The Holocaust can be a blank slate, to be scribbled on in all sorts of ways.

Back in Bobruisk, Faina said she wanted to show me some of the city's Holocaust memorials before we dropped her off at her home. There was a large selection from which to choose. When the Germans stormed through Belarus, they had still not got their innovation of mass gassings in the camps up and running. The Einsatzgruppen, the mobile killing squads, did their lethal work on the spot, and there were memorials marking many of the crime scenes.

We stopped only briefly at several of them, just enough time for Faina to deliver the relevant facts (the historical context) and figures (the number of victims). She was in hands-off mode, expressing little emotion about what she was relating. Even the most grisly history failed to produce a trace of emotion. One memorial included blocks of coal that had once been human remains. In their frantic final retreat, trying to eradicate evidence of their crimes, the Germans had burned the corpses they had not had time to bury. This information, too, Faina delivered dispassionately.

Our final stop was on the outskirts of town, at the end of a dirt path that took us past some farm fields and then a dreary institutional-looking complex of buildings.

"Mental hospital," Faina said, as if noting no more than a change in the weather.

Some of the inmates were out in the fields with pitchforks and shovels, but they only stood around in clusters, looking out into the middle distance. The notion of work had obviously escaped them. I was about to remark on this example of the fragility of human memory and link it to the need for Holocaust memorials, but Faina's demeanor told me that there was no point. We were moving with businesslike efficiency, checking items off a list as quickly as possible.

The memorial by the mental hospital had an interesting feature—two stars, one the Star of David and the other the Red Star of the Soviet Union, marked the adjoining mass graves. Several hundred Red Army POWs were buried here along with several hundred Jews. In strictly numerical terms, it made sense to have both stars. But that didn't factor in the murderers' intent. The POWs were killed because the Germans didn't mind committing war crimes. The Jews were killed as the result of a policy that viewed them as a cancer on the thousand-year Reich. But Faina was content to point out the two stars without comment.

When we got back to the city center, and just before we dropped her off, Faina began talking about her experiences during the war, and now I understood why she could appear so detached when looking at memorials.

"The Germans marched into Bobruisk so soon after the war started that there was no time to prepare. My brother, he was three, he even left without shoes, so that my mother had to carry him the whole way. At one point we had to walk on a highway, and then a German plane came by and started shooting. My mother had to make a quick decision: She could only carry my brother and push the pram I was in. She couldn't take care of my sister also. Me and my brother and mother made it to safety, eventually to Tashkent, where we spent the war. My sister died on that highway."

How could blocks of stone or a plaque commemorate that singular experience? Memorials are not up to conveying the intricate meaning of such a personal event. The choice Faina's mother made must have left a residue of guilt mixed with necessity that only the immediate family could comprehend.

But really, isn't it how you look at it? Facts that appear unique from one angle become aspects of a general history when looked at from another. There are, alas, numerous instances in Holocaust lore of a mother being forced to betray her maternal instincts— a mother smothering her baby so as not to reveal their hiding place, a mother required by the Nazis to choose which child would live and which would go to the gas chamber. Faina couldn't keep her experience uniquely personal, try as she might.

I understood Faina's predicament. At one time, I would have insisted that the circumstances of my cousin Alexandre's arrest and murder were so unusual that no public memorial could do them justice. But I was forced to admit that I was wrong.

It was some weeks before, when I had visited Berlin's Memorial to the Murdered Jews of Europe. After walking through the memorial, I had descended a stairway to the information center and spent an hour or so contemplating photographs of Jews at various points on the road to the gas chambers. I was almost ready to leave when at the very end of the exhibit something caught my eye. A note in a display case told the story of someone called Abraham Hofman. He lived on Rue de la Fraternité with his wife and four children. He owned a bakery that was doing well even after the Nazis moved in, and so he decided to remain in Paris despite the ominous rumors. Then, in July 1942, when he got word of an impending roundup, Hofman assumed it would target only adult males. He hid with his three teenage sons in his neighbors' apartment while his wife stayed with their baby boy in their apartment. He could hear his wife's cries as she and the baby were taken away. They died in Auschwitz. Hofman and his three sons survived the war.

My uncle Aronchik wasn't a baker, he didn't live on Rue de la Fraternité, and the ratio of survivors to victims didn't match. There were other differences between Aronchik and Abraham Hofman, but it was the similarities that counted, and they added up to a melancholy conclusion. The Nazis killed so many Jews, in so many different ways, that it was statistically unlikely that any one death could claim to be unique.

Later that day, after I got back to Minsk, I spoke to Tatiana on the phone and told her about the memorial I had seen on the road outside Shchedrin. She said that the existence of vampire camps was highly dubious. It was likely a wartime myth that the Soviets invented to demonize the Nazi invaders, and then it just kept going, transmuting into an afterlife that no one questioned.

Tatiana was in Minsk to attend a conference of the oral historians group she belonged to, and she invited me to the evening session. A cab took me beyond the city center, which had been totally rebuilt after the war in the grandiose late Stalinist style, and to a neighborhood of modest houses and homespun shops. The peripheral setting suited the occasion. The oral historians group operated on the edges of government-approved academe. The proceedings at the meeting were in Belarusian, not Russian, which these days qualified as an antiestablishment gesture.

With the help of Tatiana's translation, I eked out a sense of the political urgency in the main speaker's talk. A few days before, a museum exhibit organized by this group had been closed down by the authorities. No reason was given, but everyone at the conference assumed that the theme, *Belarus in 1939*, was non grata. The Molotov-Ribbentrop Pact of that year remains an explosive topic in these parts, one the government prefers to have lie dormant. Among other clauses, the pact gave the Red Army a free hand to move into all parts of Belarus, brushing aside any institutions of Polish authority.

After the talk, there was a film featuring interviews with peasants who had lived through that time. One woman says, "When the Red Army came in, they said it was to liberate their little Slavic brothers from the Poles. Yes, they liberated us. They liberated our cows, they liberated our land, they liberated our money—so much liberation that nothing was left for us."

One aim of the campaign was to clear the area of ethnic Poles, many of whom had settled in Belarus after the post–World War I partition ceded to Poland territory that was once part of the Russian Empire. But in that chaotic moment, no one was checking IDs very carefully. Among those exiled to Siberia and Kazakhstan were thousands of Jews.

The film and the discussion that followed made me understand that building a memorial to imaginary children whose blood was allegedly taken by the Nazis was a good strategy for a government beholden to Moscow, as the current Belarusian government is. Demonizing the Nazi invaders as vampires deflected attention from Russia's sins in Belarus.

When the meeting was over, twenty or so participants adjourned to a neighborhood restaurant, and they invited me to join them. We ate, we drank, we discussed the pros and cons of our two countries, the tally somehow adding up to a tie, and I was reminded of what I liked about the time I had spent in Brezhnev's Russia—the wry humor of those who lived on society's margins, the acceptance of bad odds, the determination to keep going because keeping going was the only choice.

At one point, someone asked why I was in Belarus, and I explained my project. When I mentioned how I had been fooled by the vampire memorial outside Shchedrin, there was some good-natured joking at my naïveté. I let the judgment stand without arguing. The conviviality around the table left no room for deep philosophical discussion, but really there was more I wanted to say.

Looking at that memorial, I had felt deep relief that Alexandre had been spared having his blood stolen for use by German soldiers. The vampire memorial may have been built on fantasy, but my reaction—gratitude that Alexandre had been spared an ultimate barbarity—had been authentic.

So how does that work? Is there a stable of pent-up anger and grief regarding the Holocaust and it doesn't matter what opens the door for the emotions to come galloping out? That can't be right. If memorials prompt you to feel only what you already feel, what is the difference between a good and a bad memorial?

Still, I found it impossible to discount my reaction to that faux memorial on the road outside Shchedrin. It sparked feelings about Alexandre's ordeal as powerful as any I had experienced on my trip. I had felt what I had felt.

There is a Holocaust memorial in Nesvizh, the birthplace of Alexandre's and my grandfather Lev Ripp. It honors the July 22, 1941, uprising in the local ghetto. There were only a few such uprisings during all of the war, and critics who argue for an inherent passivity in the Jewish character have stressed that fact, almost always invidiously. Facing certain death, why not die fighting? But really the better question is not why there were few uprisings but why there were any.

The Germans' strategy was meant to block resistance before it could get going. When an *aktion* was imminent and resistance most likely, all able-bodied men were sent out of the ghetto on a purported work detail and then shot and buried in a pit. The remaining ghetto population, of old men, women, and children, all usually weakened by malnutrition and disease, could be easily controlled.

And yet there were ghetto insurrections. But they required very particular circumstances. The Warsaw Ghetto Uprising of April 1943 is a case in point. Most of the older leadership of the Jewish community fled Warsaw before the ghetto was established, leaving a younger and more militant generation to fill the vacuum. Some had served in the Polish army, giving them military and organizational skills. Others belonged to Betar, the youth group that had for years been arguing for Jews to organize into self-defense units. Perhaps most important, there were links to the resistance movement outside the ghetto, especially to the Polish Home Army. The promise of weapons—whether fulfilled or not, an issue that is still argued—provided confidence for a showdown with the Nazis.

None of these conditions existed in the Nesvizh ghetto. Nevertheless, the Jews there stood and fought. The decisive factor may well have been that they had a particular history that sustained them. Weapons and some military-style organization would have helped more, but a particular history was better than nothing.

I'm relying on the memoirs of Morris Cohen, who grew up in Nesvizh. He subsequently immigrated to America and became a well-regarded philosopher at the City College of New York. He was the recipient of numerous academic prizes, and the Cohen Library on the CCNY campus is named in his honor. Though I know nothing of his philosophical work, I'm going to assume he's a reliable observer. If you can't trust a philosopher to be accurate, whom can you trust?

Cohen's description of Nesvizh in the early twentieth century stresses the absence of things. The streets were unpaved and unlighted. The wooden houses were undersized and the ventilation inadequate. Lack of adequate water made disease common and ensured that any fire would be a calamity. It sounds awful. But according to Cohen, the Jews of Nesvizh were not despondent. This seems to have been in large part because they believed there were others worse off. Cohen notes the low opinion the Jews had for any non-Jew they encountered. Most of these were lower-class townspeople and ex-serfs who lived in the countryside, whose lack of an education gave Jews a reason to feel superior. But the low opinion extended to all non-Jews, educated or not. Consider this comment by Cohen: "I remember that among us children there was a separate set of words to characterize the life cycle of non-Jews. Since, in our eyes, they did not have a proper religious ceremony, they did not marry; they mated. Their children, according to our manner of speech, were not born; they were brought into the world the way cattle are. So, too, they did not die; they passed away like the beasts of the field."*

Because non-Jews were stupid, they were like oxen. Because they lacked the right religion, they were as bereft of spirituality as cows. Jews might have been at a disadvantage politically and socially, but they were superior in what counted.

Cohen relates an episode involving a regiment of tsarist cavalry that was encamped near Nesvizh. One night the soldiers

*Morris Raphael Cohen. *A Dreamer's Journal*, 28–29.

attacked a Jewish inn on the outskirts of town and killed several Jews. Cohen's reaction: "As far as I can recall, that . . . did not arouse any fear in me." His placid response made sense. The attack was a normal feature of the natural world, as when a jungle tiger attacks its prey not out of malice but for nutrition. You have to accept the world as it is. The way to deal with such a force as the tsarist cavalry was to stay out of its way.

In the twentieth century, Nesvizh was consecutively under the authority of Poles, Soviets, and Nazis, but for the town's Jews it would have been reasonable to place them all in the same category of beasts of the field and to avoid them as much as possible. When it became impossible to avoid the Nazis, it was crucial to remember their nature. The Nazis presented themselves as rational, all their commands aimed at efficiency and order. But Nesvizh's history suggested they were a blind, malevolent force who would kill Jews without conscience.

In October 1941, several days after the Wehrmacht took control of Nesvizh, all Jews were ordered to report to the courtyard of the Radziwill castle for a routine document check. Professionals, including engineers, doctors, blacksmiths, and tailors, among others, were ordered confined to the recently established ghetto. The stated reason was that they had skills that the Germans required. But the effect was to sequester those most likely to resist the invaders. In fact, most of the remaining population, including young children, was immediately marched to a wood outside of town and slaughtered by an Einsatzgruppen detachment.

Several weeks later, the ghetto was ordered evacuated under the pretense of resettlement. The Jews would be transported to areas where their skills would best be put to use. But many in the ghetto resisted the order and stood and fought—from uncommon bravery but also thanks to the knowledge that the town's history provided. Though resettlement might have seemed a reasonable plan, Nesvizh's Jews understood that the Nazis' goals were invariably vicious. They were like beasts of the field.

From Minsk, it was two hours by bus to Nesvizh. Nearing our destination, the driver announced that we would disembark at a temporary terminal. The permanent one was *na remont*. I had a tremor of unease. The phrase was familiar to me from the year I lived in Leningrad. Literally it translates as "under repair," but in those dreary Soviet days when a lot of jobs were just make-work, it usually meant something like "gone fishing."

The temporary terminal, at the far edge of town, reeked of alcohol and sadness. The clerk brushed off my query about the return-trip schedule with a shrug. Instead, she undertook a deep reading of some sort of interoffice memo. It *was* like the old Soviet Union, when clerks and salesgirls and restaurant doormen looked forward to queries just for the chance to ignore them.

She did finally give me directions to the town center, grudgingly. They were laconic to the point of prophecy. Walk along the highway before turning into a park. Follow the curving path through the woods. Keep walking till you see a castle.

First I walked farther than felt right. The path I turned onto proved to be a dead end. Doubling back, I found a way through a dark and dense wood that could have been a park, depending on your definition. This was taking longer than I expected, and I began to worry I would miss the last bus back to Minsk. I began to sweat. I didn't want to get stuck in this godforsaken place.

The Radziwill castle appeared with fairy-tale abruptness. A break in the trees. A burst of sunlight. A large shimmering lake in the foreground and then a majestic turreted construction surrounded by a moat. There was, I was sure, nothing like this in all of Belarus.

Getting closer, I saw that what from afar had an austere grandeur was overwhelmed by a Coney Island–style commotion. There were tourists everywhere, all armed with cameras. Owners of souvenir stands hawked their wares. An ice cream cart advertised six flavors. And, what most caught my eye, several boisterous wedding parties. The newly married couples were seated in horse-driven carriages with celebrants walking and singing and drinking alongside. It must have seemed like a good idea in the planning, but in the event, with four or five carriages in danger of jostling one another, the image that came to mind was bumper cars in a boardwalk concession.

I went into the courtyard of the castle, where the Germans had forced Jews to gather before being marched off to the ghetto. None of the tourists paused here as they headed to the castle's entrance. Tatiana had told me the interior was not worth the price of admission. It had been looted by the Red Army when they drove out the Germans, and so far, despite many promises, what had been taken had not been returned. But that wasn't why I didn't go inside. Of course not every vestige of the Holocaust should stop you in your tracks. The past sometimes should stay in the past. But it would have taken a high degree of moral blindness to go without pause from where the Nazis had readied Jews for slaughter to a stroll amid the ornaments of aristocratic comfort.

I never did find the Holocaust memorial that I had come to see. To tell the truth, I didn't spend much time looking for it. I had seen a photo of the memorial, and the inscription on the plinth indicated that the memorial was erected in honor of the fifteen hundred Soviet citizens who had died at the hands of the Nazis. I wasn't going to risk missing the last bus to Minsk just to see one more of those sleights of hand that made thousands of Jewish victims disappear by folding them into the suffering of the Soviet homeland.

On the bus ride back, I groused to myself about having made a trip with nothing much to show for it except a reminder that life can be narrow and bleak. From the sullen clerk at the bus terminal to the oblivious tourists marching across the courtyard, human decency seemed in short supply. But then something happened that eased my gloomy mood.

Two teenage girls kept asking the driver to stop so they could pee. He grumpily refused, citing company policy. He kept his eyes on the road and his posture soldier-stiff. The bus was his domain and he would rule over it as he saw fit. But then after thirty minutes or so, because of what I could only think of as grace descending, he pulled off onto the shoulder in the middle of nowhere, and the girls disappeared into the nearby woods. Over and done in a minute, and we were back on the road. The face of common humanity didn't show up very often in these parts, but when it did it had a sweet power. Perhaps some sympathy for Jewish victims of the Holocaust also broke through the general indifference from time to time.

Minsk is the setting for one of the iconic anecdotes about the Holocaust. The cruelty that it describes is so medieval that it makes you wonder if the facts aren't concocted. Twenty or so very young Jewish children were thrown into a deep sand pit to suffocate. Present was SS officer Wilhelm Kube, in immaculate dress uniform and wearing white gloves. In response to the children's shrieks and pleas, he coolly threw them some candy. Two weeks later, Kube's Belarusian maid hid a bomb disguised as a water bottle under his bed. On hearing that Kube had been killed, Himmler noted that he had anyway been insufficiently enthusiastic in carrying out his duty to destroy Minsk's Jewish population. There had always been some doubt about Kube in Nazi circles because he called himself a practicing Christian. This has everything one could want in a Holocaust anecdote. Innovative cruelty. The revenge of the weak upon the strong. Himmler's calculus of brutality. A stone-cold killer advertising his religious beliefs. But I'm fairly certain it is the image of those suffocating children that holds most people's attention. It does mine. Stories of Nazi sadism can be like pornography, disgusting but hard to turn away from, and as with pornography, what should be moral judgment becomes mere curiosity. Better to concentrate on memorials, I told myself. They don't have that kind of dangerous ambiguity. There was one in Minsk I had planned to see, and now I was even more eager. I wanted some way to think of the city other than as Kube's monstrous playground.

Minsk's downtown is urban planning gone off the rails. The boulevards are built so wide that I had to run to reach the other side before the light changed red. The heavy traffic lurches forward like a stolid beast, indifferent to pedestrians. Tall, sleek buildings beetle over the crowded sidewalks.

The giant dimensions of the neighborhood overwhelmed my sense of direction, and I had to stop every five minutes and consult my map. Finally, I decided to take a taxi to get to Minsk's most famous Holocaust memorial—famous according to the guidebooks, less so among the citizenry. It was only because I knew the names of the cross streets that the cabbie figured out my destination. He dropped me near a patch of grass and trees, with no memorial in view. When I asked a passerby, she pointed me to a spot just fifty yards away. I felt stupid, like standing at the Trocadéro and asking for the location of the Eiffel Tower. But the woman assured me that most tourists were stumped when they came looking for the memorial. Signs would have helped, but maybe the government didn't want to advertise a Jewish tragedy. If that was the policy, it worked. There was no one at the memorial site but me.

The memorial, in a sunken space below street level, comprises some forty square feet of cobblestone paving. At one end there's a commemorative plaque: "In holy memory of the five million Jews who died at the hands of ferocious enemies of humanity, the Fascistic German monsters." That's a case of one hand giving what the other takes away. The inscription recognizes Jews as particular victims of the Nazis, which is rare for a Soviet-era memorial. But in referring to fascism it subsumes the Holocaust to a conflict between political ideologies. Most Jews would have been surprised to learn they were murdered for their belief in communism. The plaque was installed in 1947, when the Soviet Union was especially determined to spread the Marxist-Leninist word.

The section of the memorial at the other end, a collaboration between a local artist and an Israeli sculptor, was added in 2001 and is less ideologically combative. It's here that the title of the memorial—"the Pit" (*Iama*)—is given a form, calling to mind the Nazis' practice of shooting Jews as they stood at the lip of open trenches that would serve as mass graves. Twenty bronze figures, representing young children, a pregnant woman, a baby, and an old man, as well as adult males, are set on the incline at the edge of the space. They are highly stylized, Giacometti-like, and their spindly torsos are contorted to suggest spiritual agony as well as physical pain. This is a representation of the last few moments before oblivion encompasses them. There is no hint of any redemption. Nothing any of them did in their lives stands against their imminent fate.

But by starting from the bottom of the row of human-like figures and walking up the steps that run alongside, as I did, you see two stages of an argument, thesis and antithesis. Though there is a depiction of Jewish tragedy, that tragedy is transcended. This logic becomes clear when you reach the last figure in the line—a man playing a fiddle, which he holds at such a jaunty angle that he must be playing a triumphant tune.

Marc Chagall was born in Vitebsk, not far from Minsk, and it was Chagall who made the figure of a Jewish fiddler famous— though of course it was the Broadway show *Fiddler on the Roof* that multiplied the icon's popularity. But geography only partly explains the presence of a fiddler in the memorial.

Though not deeply religious himself, Chagall was influenced by the Hasidic revival of his time, and more particularly by the Hasidic emphasis on the power of music. Music could express what was otherwise inexpressible. It was a way to see beyond the misery of the Diaspora. Ecstatic dancing, often to fiddle music, revealed a vision of the divine that the material world usually disguised. It was this set of beliefs that makes the fiddler on the Minsk memorial appropriate. He is a symbol of a religious perspective that can accommodate even the Holocaust.

In Shchedrin, the shtetl where my grandmother Zina grew up, everything was subordinated to religion. First thing in the morning, there was synagogue. Then the men went to the office and the boys to cheder to study the Talmud. The midday meal was at noon, tea at four. Then the synagogue again. The women went to the mikvah, the ritual bath, as the religious calendar required. Most evenings, Zina's father read the Torah.

Though religious law determined much of daily life in Shchedrin, it wasn't the only way conduct was controlled. In her taped recollections, Zina emphasized the importance of "the book." That was where any out-of-the-ordinary event was recorded. If a young woman had an accident that might subsequently put her virginity into question, that went into the book. If a married couple argued and the husband spent the night in the stable, that went into the book.

The shtetl elders controlled the contents of the book, and this gave them broad authority. No one wanted to have his or her behavior displayed for public curiosity. The elders could, if so inclined, shape public behavior to suit themselves. That was the case in one instance that especially provoked Zina.

"My grandfather was a big aesthete, he had many hats, all with fine fur, very luxurious. He built himself a big house with expensive furniture. He had horses and a lackey and went riding every day. He allowed singing at the dinner table. But at the same time he forbade women from strolling with men. If someone complained, saying, 'What about a woman walking with her husband?' he would answer, 'I don't want to always have to check who is with who—just let men be with men and women with women always.'"

An evening stroll was the main diversion in Shchedrin, every day but the Sabbath. It was a cherished break from the rule-bound days. When Zina's grandfather proclaimed that women could not walk with men, there was wide dismay. Zina's was compounded by what she saw as her grandfather's duplicity. He indulged himself with pleasures but insisted that others live up to a strict code.

Zina said, "And that's how it was. No men and women strolling together. Well, that's how it was except when he was taking a nap. Then men and women would stroll together." I could make out a note of satisfaction when Zina mentioned this small victory against hypocrisy.

Because of the book, even more than because of religious law, daily life in Shchedrin was oppressive. Zina said, "You couldn't do anything without everyone knowing it. Life inside the shtetl was suffocating. Many, especially the young men, wanted to leave.

Life outside seemed promising, you could maybe get an education, find a good job."

Indeed, though most Jews were confined to the Pale of Settlement, that restriction could be circumvented. The government's elaborate network of rules was often haphazardly enforced—an enterprising Jew could cut his *peyot*, discard his distinctive clothing, get hold of a forged passport, and move to Saint Petersburg or Moscow. Once there, one had to prove gainful employment, but with a bit of ingenuity that ploy could be carried out.

Zina said, "I had a relative who managed to get to Moscow, where he claimed he was a tailor. He always walked around with a tape measure around his neck and carrying an ironing board. If a policeman questioned him, he just pointed to his tools of the trade. Several others I knew said they were printers. If they were stopped, they showed their ink-stained hands."

Zina was well aware of the world beyond Shchedrin. She spoke Russian in addition to Yiddish, she looked at the "thick journals," the influential platforms of the intelligentsia, that occasionally came into her hands. But to leave Shchedrin, she had to wait for the mandated route of marriage. She returned only once, and then briefly, to give birth to her son. She was glad to have left behind a life tightly constricted by authority, whether defined by Jewish law or by the shtetl elders. But also, with no sense of contradiction, she remembered her shtetl years as a time of happiness. Even the religious practices, which she had once found so constraining, now appeared to her to have some good in them.

She told this anecdote: "My mother was a passionate believer, even beyond Orthodox. When my father became very sick, she took me and my younger sister to synagogue to say a prayer. As if talking directly to my father, she said, 'You cannot leave our children as orphans. I don't ask for me but for them—give us another ten years.' And that is what happened, he lived for exactly ten more years. And, you know, though it seems ridiculous, I am glad my mother went to the synagogue and prayed. Did it really help? You never can tell."

One of my lasting images of my grandmother is of her lighting the Sabbath candles in her Manhattan apartment, covering her eyes with her hands and murmuring a prayer. If she ever saw me watching, she didn't acknowledge my presence. She was completely attentive to her own world.

Thinking back, I now realize that Zina must surely have prayed like that all through her life, including when the Kahans were trying to escape the Nazis. I don't think she was ever any more a believer than when she was in Shchedrin, but why not pray? You never can tell.

When I was still in the States and making hotel reservations in Grodno, Tatiana had steered me away from the hotel I had found on the Internet. "*Pafosnyi*," she had declared in an e-mail. Literally, that is "enthusiastic," but in Tatiana's rendering it came out as "glitzy" and "sophisticated," but not in a good way. The hotel I ended up at on her recommendation was definitely not *pafosnyi*. The desk clerk was oblivious, the furniture in my dimly lit room was end-of-life dowdy, the complimentary soap was doled out in one tiny packet per day.

To balance that, in Minsk I stayed at a five-star hotel. Each morning, to get to the buffet breakfast, I had to nudge my way around the members of a Chinese trade mission. None smiled, none acknowledged my "Excuse me." Every evening when I returned to the hotel, I was eyed suspiciously by the hotel's high-powered security detail. Inexplicably, the small safe in my room never worked, though I complained several times.

I was never comfortable in either hotel, as I was never entirely comfortable anywhere in Belarus. This was my ancestral home-land, but except for one or two random moments I didn't feel the magic. It's been said of Russia that it is a country for which you feel nostalgic even when you are right there, and I felt the same way about Belarus. It had been satisfying tracking down my family to its beginnings, and I was glad to have come. But I was ready to leave.

My flight was at 4:00 a.m. on Belair, the national airline. Or-dinarily I would have been annoyed by the odd schedule, but now the sooner I said goodbye to Belarus, the better. When I got to the airport, I learned my flight was canceled. No apologies, no explanation why there had been no notification of a delay. A grumpy agent put me on a flight that was scheduled to depart six hours later. One last time that my desire and Belarus's response didn't match up.

I tried to put the wait time to good use by reading up on the next memorial I planned to see. I was headed back to Germany, to Hamburg. There was a memorial there designed by Jochen Gerz, an artist with a well-articulated theory of public memori-als. This is what he told a reporter from *Art Times*: "Traditional monuments are kitsch . . . If you are representing an absence, you create an absence. That same absence also permits each per-son [who visits the memorial] to become the author of his or her own memorial."*

Gerz had put his theory into practice in Harburg, a suburb of Hamburg. His memorial was a forty-foot-high lead-coated column with an attached instrument that allowed passersby to inscribe messages on the column. As inscriptions were added, the column gradually descended into the ground. There was an explanatory text near the column: "We invite the citizens of

*Jochen Gerz, www.youtube.com.

Harburg and visitors to add their names next to ours. In doing so, we commit ourselves to remain vigilant. As more and more names are added to the column, it will gradually descend into the ground. One day it will have disappeared completely, and the site of the Harburg Monument Against Fascism will be empty. In the end it is only we ourselves who can stand up against injustice."

I looked forward to seeing Gerz's memorial, given his unusual ideas. I recalled something the critic Northrop Frye had said: Books are like a picnic. The author brings the words and the reader brings the meanings. Gerz presumably would have agreed that his memorial was a kind of picnic. He had supplied the notion of remembrance and with that he had done his part. It was up to the visitor to bring some meaning with which to fill in that notion.

I wondered how that would work.

I put up at a hotel in downtown Hamburg, not far from the harbor. From there it was a forty-five-minute ride on the S-Bahn to the suburb of Harburg. My plan was that once there I would ask someone to direct me to Gerz's memorial. I exited the station into a cut-rate mall and stopped in at a few shops, but no one knew what I was talking about. Finally, I found a police station and went in to inquire. The officers on duty were excited to learn such a memorial existed in their town.

I had assumed I would have no trouble finding the memorial, even though by this time it had completely descended into the ground. Gerz's description suggested that his memorial held the continual attention of Harburg's citizens, a perpetual civics lesson that they had volunteered to keep studying. But apparently once the memorial was no longer visible, the locals, like schoolkids let out for summer recess, found more pleasant ways to spend their time.

I finally stumbled upon the memorial, or at least the sign indicating where it had once been. Two elements were still visible. On the top level there was a platform with a metal plaque covering the shaft into which the memorial had descended. On a lower level there was a small window through which it was possible to view a section of the memorial. I decided to do as Gerz suggested—to make myself the author of my own memorial.

I had seen memorials that made me think about Aronchik in various ways. As an innocent trying to figure out French political life, as a man bewildered by Vichy policies, as a loving father—in all cases, looking through the prism of a memorial had charged his life with tragic meaning. So how would it work if a memorial did nothing but invite me to provide my own memory of Aronchik?

The only time I saw Aronchik was in Paris in 1949, when my family returned for a triumphant tour of the land where we had been hounded and threatened. But the occasion was clouded by Aronchik's poor health. He was confined to bed, suffering from a sickness from which he would never recover. He had survived the Nazis only to die not too long after they had been kicked out.

I had never seen anyone so close to death, and I think it was to try to soften the shock that my father recounted Aronchik's life during the occupation as an adventure. It had been, my father said, full of risk-taking and offhand courage. I shouldn't be misled by how he looked now. Aronchik's pallor and weakness said nothing about who he really was—that seemed to be the strategy holding together my father's anecdotes.

For most of the occupation, Aronchik lived in the back room of the Kahan business office on Rue de la Bienfaisance in the Eighth Arrondissement, choosing a hiding place in the city center although one in an outlying neighborhood would have been safer. The Union Générale des Israélites de France, which often acted as an arm of the German occupation, was on the same street. Friends brought him food, but he ventured out on his own for other items.

Occasionally, he went to a friend's house to play cards. If he missed the curfew, he would sleep in his friend's bathtub. One particular desire during those years was to ride the Métro, just to be reminded of a normal life no longer available. That was a very risky pleasure. There were spot checks for proper documents, and there was no escape once the Gestapo came aboard and began a methodical, person-by-person pat-down. He actually did ride the Métro once. As I said, my father wanted to make it sound thrilling.

When I saw Aronchik, he was coughing up blood that blotted the sheets, and my father had to cradle him to get him to sit upright. It was impossible for me to think of him as the hero of an adventure. I couldn't have put it into words then, but later in life I would have said that Aronchik was reduced to his biological body. Looking at him through the prism of a memorial had given him some social heft, some qualities that placed him in a defined historical moment, but looking at him directly I saw none of that. He appeared merely human, and that wasn't enough to provide him with the dignity that his tragic story deserved.

From my Hamburg hotel, it was a short ride on the U-Bahn to the Altona section of the city. I exited the station into a sedate neighborhood. Kreigerstrasse, the main thoroughfare, was lined with unexceptional residential houses and a few nondescript shops. I felt I had arrived at ground zero of Hamburg's middle class, programmed for conventional bourgeois comfort. But then the vista opened up onto a lush park approximately the size of a football field that suggested a more expansive view of life. The park was divided into three sections by walkways and hedges. At the end of one of the sections stood City Hall, and in front of that a Holocaust memorial created by Sol LeWitt.

LeWitt seems a curious choice to design a Holocaust memorial. He is famous for geometric constructions devoid of any emotional charge. Some of his comments about his work sound more like those of a draftsman on a public works job than an artist caught up in the throes of creation: "All of the planning and decisions are made beforehand and the execution is a perfunctory affair. The idea becomes a machine that makes the art . . . [The artist] would want [the work] to be emotionally dry."*

LeWitt's memorial was a cast concrete block painted black, eighteen feet long, six feet high, and six feet wide. My first thought was that it looked like a crypt. But that would have contradicted LeWitt's vision. His work, he had said, might as well have been generated by a machine. A crypt is a poetic image, and machines don't do poetry.

Looking closer, I saw that the block had delineated rectangles on its surface, each about one foot by six inches and arranged in eight rows. The pattern was unchanging across the surface, so lacking in deviation that it seemed there was no logical reason it should stop. Indeed, some rows ended with an incomplete rectangle, implying that the pattern might have extended to infinity but for the physical limit of the block. That notion—that the meaning of the memorial exceeds what its physical form can encompass—struck me as an elegant representation of the fact that the number of Jewish victims exceeds human comprehension.

When I looked into my camera viewfinder, I noticed something else. Directly behind the memorial was City Hall, rebuilt after the war in the high Baroque style of the original. In front of City Hall, on a high pedestal, was a statue of Kaiser Wilhelm I on horseback, surrounded by figures representing the traditional occupations of the citizens of Altona—fishermen, craftsmen,

*Sol LeWitt. "Paragraphs on Conceptual Art." *Artforum.*

again in Baroque detail. This piece of civic statuary was balanced at the other end of the park by a statue of Triton battling a sea serpent. The contrast between the sleek modernism of LeWitt's memorial and the ornate traditionalism in which it was set was jarring. The memorial didn't fit in, and though unintended, that incongruity made a telling point. Jews in Hamburg had learned to their dismay that they didn't fit in. They thought they were integrated into the civic life, but then the Nazis came and showed them that they could be easily removed.

The wording on a plaque near the memorial unintentionally underscores that point. It reads "Black Form. Dedicated to the missing Jews." As a German friend told me later when I asked, this mistranslates the German words on the same plaque: The phrase *"Juden die für immer fehlen"* refers to Jews *who are forever missed*, emphasizing the regret and sense of loss among those who contemplate the Jewish tragedy. But it seemed to me that the English wording, mistranslation that it was, actually fits the facts better. It suggests how the inhabitants of Hamburg were used to seeing Jews everywhere in their city, and then when they looked again, all the Jews were gone.

The next day, I went to the Altona Museum, where two rooms were devoted to the history of Jews in Hamburg. Walking through the exhibit made me understand how surprised the city's Jews must have felt when they were deported. For a long time they had been respected citizens. They were given legal equality in the early nineteenth century, sooner than in many other parts of Europe. Altona had a reputation for tolerance, partly because it was first settled by Danes, who brought with them their liberal tradition. The Jews, for their part, were eager to integrate. In the early nineteenth century, Hamburg was a center of the Reform movement, which aimed to make Judaism more fully a part of the surrounding culture.

The exhibit includes a model of a typical middle-class Jewish apartment in the early twentieth century. Visitors are free to walk in and have a closer look. I sat down in an armchair, sinking into its deep cushions. Across the room was a polished mahogany chest. To my left there was a case with shelves of books with worn leather bindings that suggested they had been read and reread many times. All the furniture was sturdy, heavy. The effect was of an abiding immobility. This furniture was meant to stay where it was put, and in this it was a perfect symbol of the Hamburg Jews' belief that they had found a permanent home. But it turned out that the Nazis held the lease, and the Jews could be evicted at their whim.

It takes, I think, a particular cast of mind to grasp the fact that one is only a transient in a country where one has lived happily for decades. Many German Jews of the interwar period failed to understand this. They spoke the language without accent, they admired the kaiser, they loved Wagner. What further proof was needed that they belonged? But then they were kicked out of their homes, many of them ending up in the killing camps.

The Kahans occupied a particular position in German society, both inside and outside, and that gave them a perspective that most German Jews lacked. But it also mattered that their previous life in Baku had taught them what it was like to be only precariously connected with the society in which they lived. For that kind of ambiguous status, the more practice the better.

The Kahans had come to Baku carrying with them European rationality and good manners, not the best survival tools in a city of long-standing tribal and ethnic rivalries. Though they managed to carve out a life for themselves, they never settled in. When they moved to Germany, they came with the knowledge that though a place could look and feel like home, that didn't mean you were guaranteed lifetime occupancy.

My mother was born in Baku in 1909 and left in 1920. What she remembered most vividly were the summers. The heat, she said, was stifling. Blackflies swarmed. The city's water supply was undependable. It rarely rained, but when it did, the streets turned to mud. Wealthier citizens could hire a man who would carry them on his back across the street. And then there was the wind off the Caspian—*Baku* is Persian for "Cradle of the Wind." In the summer, the wind never stopped.

My mother said, "It could drive you crazy. I think that's why there were so many riots in the summer."

In fact, riots in Baku went on year-round, though maybe there were fewer outside the summer months. The population of the city was ethnically diverse, but not in a good way. Along with a small community of Jews, there were Armenians, Azeris, Persians, Russians, and various local tribes. Each of these groups worshipped a different god, one who was quick to demand revenge for any insult, real or imagined.

Though it's not precisely on target, when I think of my family's life in Baku, I can't help but recall a remark by Alexander Pushkin. In *A Journey to Arzrum*, a record of his travels to Transcaucasia, Pushkin described his encounter with a local tribesman taken prisoner for shooting at a Russian soldier: "He tried to defend himself by claiming that his rifle had been loaded for too long. What is one to do with such a people?"* Pushkin's journey was in 1829 and it was to a different region of Transcaucasia, but it seemed to me true that when the Kahans lived in Baku, its inhabitants were also very quick to reach for their weapons. An accidental jostle in the marketplace and the knives would come out.

Atypically in the long and sad saga of ethnic and religious

*A. S. Pushkin. "Puteshestvie v Arzrum."

hatreds in the Russian Empire, Jews were not the target. The antagonism among the various other groups kept them busy. The Kahans' strategy was mainly to keep their heads down and avoid the crossfire. In 1918 there was a weeklong riot between the Azeris and the Armenians. One wealthy Armenian was under siege in his house just down the street from the Kahans.

This is the way my mother remembered the event: "We hid in the cellar of our building for three days, not coming up except to go to the bathroom. Luckily it was Passover, and some food had been stored in the cellar. For three days we ate pickles and marinated salmon on matzoh."

In their business dealings, the Kahans sometimes had contact with the non-Jewish world around them, though they kept this to a minimum. Socially they tried to stay within their own circle. My mother went to a school for Jewish girls that was founded by several local wealthy Jews. She had a French governess, her brother had a German tutor. The family had a live-in cook and a seamstress who came almost every day. For daily purchases they went to the marketplace, but they did their serious shopping abroad. Furniture from Berlin, books from Vilnius, clothes from Warsaw—the "Paris of the East," as it was known in those days. My grandmother Zina spent her days soliciting donations for Jewish charities, moving money from more prosperous Jews to less prosperous ones, a self-contained circulation of Jewish wealth.

It was relatively easy for the Kahans to stay aloof in business, and even personal encounters could be controlled, but there were hundreds of ordinary moments when the world intruded. In my mother's telling, the world intruded for her almost as soon as she was born.

"Our apartment at the time was on the promenade near to the harbor. That was a largely Tartar neighborhood," my mother said, using the vernacular for the city's Azeri population. "The first word I remember hearing was 'ris,' which was Tartar for 'iris.' It was a kind of candy, and the Tartar kids would run through the streets trying to sell it. Other memories from that time? The laundry lines strung across our narrow street from one balcony to another. And the smells from the bazaar around the corner."

Though my mother didn't intend it, she had delivered a neat symbol for the situation of the Kahans in Baku—indicating how the sounds and images and odors of an alien culture kept coming in as if through a slightly open window.

Life was a series of cultural accommodations, more or less successful. "I would be walking in the market and there would be the sound of the muezzin. Muslim men would suddenly fall to their knees, it was the hour of prayer. That's not something I could ignore, just to walk around the men as if they were tree stumps."

But it wasn't only that the Kahans looked upon the surrounding culture as strange. They could never forget that the surrounding culture looked back at them and found them equally strange. Though the Kahans did not wear distinctive Jewish clothing or yarmulkes or otherwise advertise their religion, they still stood out in Baku's roiling sea of Muslims, Christians, and Russian Orthodox. They moved differently, they spoke differently, they had different holidays. The family rule of thumb was: Nothing can make you invisible, but don't call attention to yourself, just go about your business.

The only family member who didn't abide by the rule was my grandfather Pinchas. He didn't only ignore the rule, he flouted his disapproval. His philosophy was that there was no hiding from the world. Indeed, hadn't Baku accepted the family, as witness the fact that the Kahans were never harmed and were allowed to prosper? A balance had been struck, Pinchas claimed. Withdrawing into a shell would only unsettle things.

Every night after the evening meal, Pinchas put on his dinner jacket and left the house. The family had moved to Nicolaevsky Street, in the city's most upscale neighborhood. Directly across the street was the fashionable Summer Club, and that was Pinchas's destination. For several hours each night he played *preferans*. He never won too much money and he never lost too much either. Cardplaying was not really the point. Putting in an appearance in Baku's society was. That kept the balance.

Whether that balance was real or a myth conjured in Pinchas's imagination, it collapsed in 1920, when the civil war that followed the revolution made its way over the Caucasus. New allegiances were established, old ones discarded, and the Kahans could no longer stay on the sidelines. But their options were limited. As bourgeois industrialists, they were targets for the Communist Reds. As Jews, they were targets for the anti-Semitic Whites.

When the Red Army began moving south, my granduncle Aron knew it was time to escape—he was on a hit list for writing anticommunist articles. A concocted document bearing the seal of a nonexistent workers' organization got him past one checkpoint. The disguise of a peasant coat that doubled his girth along with a cap pulled over his face got him past another, though that was a close call—the tailor who had made the coat still kept to the old ways, and he had sewn in a silk lining such as was suitable for someone of Aron's social position. But a sack of potatoes that Aron carried over his shoulder bluffed the checkpoint guards into not looking too closely.

The escape of Zina and her children was only slightly less harrowing. Local tribes took advantage of the wartime chaos to do mischief and worse. Trains were constantly rerouted, and some lines were simply declared defunct. A key bridge was blown up, bringing all travel to a halt, and causing Zina and her children to spend one night in a mosquito-infested wood. The crossing into Georgia was by way of a rope bridge that, my mother noted, swayed back and forth with the wind. It was far from a trip *en tout confort*, such as the Kahans were used to.

Retelling these events, my mother was remarkably good-humored, even cheerful. It was, after all, an adventure that ended happily with a boat crossing from Batumi to the safety of Constantinople. The only moment she showed any anger at what she had been forced to endure was in describing her Nansen passport, the document issued by the League of Nations to those who had been rendered stateless by political catastrophes.

"It didn't even look like a real passport," she said. "It was just a green little booklet that folded up like an accordion. I was so happy when I got married and got a Polish passport. My husband hated the Poles, and so a Polish passport was not the one we would have taken if we had a choice, but at least it was issued by a real country. It wasn't a Nansen, it wasn't just a flimsy little booklet."

Once they got to America, life was accommodating enough that the Kahans were confident they would not suddenly be kicked from their homes. New York was not Baku or Berlin. But some in the family never felt perfectly in tune with the surrounding society. The best example of this was my uncle Lolia. Over the years, in many countries, he had been forced into the role of outsider looking in, and then, when he got inside, looking back with regret at what he had left behind.

When the Russian civil war came to the Transcaucasia region, Lolia was seventeen and eager for adventure. Not telling anyone in the family, he took advantage of the Whites' temporary control of Kharkov to go down to the local outpost and enlist in General Denikin's army.

Though the Whites were anticommunist, which made it reasonable for a Kahan to join them, they were also lethally anti-

Semitic. But what was a young Jew eager to play a role in his country's destiny to do? As an abstract problem, there seemed to be no answer. Practically it was solved by Alexandra Prokratina, the long-serving family nanny who had swaddled several generations of Kahans, including Lolia. She went to where he was standing sentry duty, and—as the expression had it every time I heard the story—"took him home by his collar."

During World War II, Lolia served with the British army in Palestine, fighting for a country whose anti-Jewish immigration policies had lately been codified in a white paper. David Ben-Gurion famously declared, "We must fight the war as if there were no White Paper and we must fight the White Paper as if there were no war." That was an eloquent statement of policy. But on the ground, where Lolia was, it wasn't easy fitting the two parts of the statement together.

Several years after the war, Lolia moved to America, where for a while he managed an auto repair garage in Manhattan's meatpacking neighborhood. This was before the neighborhood evolved into its current chic, and each time I brought my car in for a tune-up I saw Lolia trying to satisfy the demands of hard-nosed teamsters and aggressive New York cabbies. He held his own, but it wasn't easy. He was out of his element—his English was fine, but that didn't mean he was fluent in the local language.

There was one moment that encapsulated for me Lolia's often askew relationship with his surrounding culture. When my cousin got married, the wedding party was held at her parents' large West End Avenue apartment. It was a tumultuous affair, the center of gravity wobbling through several rooms. Each time I caught sight of Lolia, his shot glass had been refilled with vodka, but I still didn't see what was coming. Finishing off a drink in a gulp, he abruptly dropped to a squat position and executed some awkward stumbling steps of the *kazatsky*, the dance associated with the Cossacks, the eternal enemy of the Jews. And as a Cossack might do, Lolia ended his impromptu performance by throwing his shot glass in the direction of a fireplace—but there was no fireplace, just a blank wall. Everyone, me included, froze in place, shocked by this moment of high drama. Lolia wasn't drunk, though that's how it must have appeared to those used to the decorum of a typical West End Avenue party. Looking back, I see Lolia's mad dance as something else. It was a declaration that he would live with the cultural ambiguity that fate had dealt him. He would be who he had no choice but to be.

After I left the Altona Museum, I strolled down toward the embankment by the Elbe. Some fifty yards on, I found myself on a tree-lined path through a minuscule park. The street sign indicated that I was on the Betty Levi Passageway. There was a billboard with a brief biography.

Betty Levi, née Lindenberger, was born in 1908. In 1929, she met Moses Levi at the wedding party of a mutual friend. Moses was a prominent lawyer and the descendant of a line of prominent Altona rabbis. Betty was a passionate pianist, but after the marriage she devoted herself to domestic life, baking being her special talent. When the Nazis came to power, her children escaped to England on the *Kindertransport*, but she remained behind. She died in Auschwitz in 1942. The passageway in her honor was funded by one of her daughters, who prospered after coming to America.

I read the biography a second time, searching for the reason that Betty Levi merited a memorial in Hamburg's public space. Her only civic accomplishment, if you could call it that, was the connection with the line of Altona's rabbis, and that was second- or even thirdhand. It was rather Betty Levi's private life that the biography focused on—her piano playing, her cooking skills. Nothing in the bio suggested anything other than an average Hamburg hausfrau.

The contrast with the LeWitt memorial that I had seen a day earlier was stark. There, one black box stood in for millions of murdered Jews. Here, a single unremarkable woman. I studied the photo of Betty Levi that was on display. Something around the eyes suggested kindness and maybe wisdom. Her glance at the camera could be a declaration of self-satisfaction. Ultimately, however, she seemed very ordinary, and yet that was what moved me. I felt the pathos of an innocent life wantonly destroyed. So, I decided, the question wasn't if Betty Levi deserved a memorial, but rather if she deserved one any more than any other Jew who died at the hands of the Nazis. She represented no group, could not be filed away in any category. She was just who she was, and a memorial in her honor would have been fine if there were six million other memorials just like this one stretched across Europe, memorials set in every park and plaza and public walkway, so that you could hardly take a step without stumbling across a reminder of the Holocaust.

That was a good idea. People should be reminded of the Holocaust. But it was also a bad idea. Holocaust memorials shouldn't be as commonplace as Starbucks or Duane Reade, just another part of city life.

I got to Hanover by train, a ninety-minute ride from Hamburg. My guidebook noted that there was an old section of town with several architectural landmarks that were worth a visit. Hanover also has the Herrenhausen Gardens, 124 acres of lawns, hedges, and walkways that were a marvel of landscaping when laid out at the end of the seventeenth century. But I wouldn't have stopped in Hanover if Verena Dohrn hadn't lived there.

We first met because she played a major role in organizing the *Berlin Transit* exhibit at the Jewish Museum that featured the Kahan family. Now she was writing a book, in German, about the Kahan family and was already deep into her topic.

When I had visited the Jewish Museum to see the *Berlin Transit* exhibit, I was in the company of two cousins and their children. After we spent some time looking at the exhibit and the rest of the museum, we all went out into the museum garden and sat under sun umbrellas while Verena offered a brief history of the Kahan family, from its beginnings in Poland to its years in Berlin. It was odd to have someone I had never met before tell me the story of my family, especially when it was compressed into forty-five minutes—sort of a greatest-hits compendium that left out the commonplace moments in between, which gave it a kind of mythic quality.

Verena and her husband Henning met me at the Hanover train station, and we immediately drove out to see the former Israelite School of Horticulture. It was founded in 1893 in the Hanover suburb of Ahlem with the aim of teaching young Jewish men and women farming and gardening. The emphasis on practical skills was popular in interwar Germany. Jews who intended to immigrate to Palestine should be equipped to work the land of the Yishuv. The Ahlem school was exceptional because it intended that its graduates would work in Germany—at least until Nazism rendered that plan wishful thinking.

The Nazis turned the Ahlem school into a "Jew house," where Jews were imprisoned before being transported to the Riga ghetto and then on to Auschwitz and Theresienstadt. In the courtyard adjoining the main house, there is a forty-foot commemorative wall with the names of the Jews who were deported from here. One panel of the wall is devoted to Jews who committed suicide. Even at this first step of their itinerary, the final destination was obvious, so why wait? Some forty Jews took their fate into their own hands, short-circuiting the lethal process.

Another panel of the wall has the names of some of the German officers who were part of the failed conspiracy to assassinate Hitler. They were shot on these grounds, thus escaping Hitler's preferred punishment of slow-motion garroting. Their resistance to Hitler certainly makes them deserving of commemoration, but it was morally confounding to see the names of German officers in such proximity to the names of Jewish victims. Just being German officers meant they were complicit to some degree in the carrying out of the Final Solution. Surely, I thought, there was enough space in Germany to segregate victims and victimizers.

What had once been the main building of the agricultural school has been transformed into a museum. There are exhibits tracing the school's history from its beginnings. Alexander Moritz Simon was a local banker whose early life was spent within the circle of Hanover's high bourgeoisie. But in time he became aware of the slums that were home to East European Jewish immigrants. Simon, unlike many Germans of the time, insisted that their poverty came not from bad work habits but because the law blocked Jews from most well-paid jobs. His remedy was to teach Jews agricultural skills, which allowed them to multiply their occupational possibilities.

Sukkot, with its celebration of the harvest in ancient Palestine, was a holiday of particular significance for the students at the horticulture school, since the goal was that they would someday be bringing in harvests of their own. A sukkah, a temporary shelter like one that would have been erected during the forty years that the Jews wandered the desert, is an integral part of the celebration. The school made do with a shed that was on the grounds, keeping the skylights open to symbolize close contact with nature.

The Nazis had another use for the shed. They used it to carry out executions. There were some fifty victims, a minuscule number in the context of the Final Solution. But it's noteworthy as another example of the Nazis' talent for cruelty. They took a place of communal rejoicing and turned it into a killing zone. A modest memorial marks the spot.

Verena and Henning were marvelous hosts, driving me to Ahlem, providing excellent meals and lively conversation. One evening, after a postprandial stroll, our conversation quite naturally turned to the Kahan family. I knew things Verena didn't, she knew things I didn't. She could explain how the Kahans got their oil company listed on the Saint Petersburg stock exchange, no easy feat for a Jewish business in those days, she could quote the annual tonnage of the oil-carrying tankers the Kahans owned when they lived in Berlin. Her research had taken her to Warsaw, Baku, Vilnius, Saint Petersburg, and Tel Aviv, always to dig deep in the local archives. She had also found several documents in a Columbia University archive, which was particularly startling. I grew up in New York, I got a degree from Columbia, this was home territory. Verena's discoveries in the Columbia archive felt like a commando raid on my past, come and gone before I even knew there was anything worth taking.

Verena's research spanned a lot of geography, but she was also intent on covering the full chronology of the Kahans' story from its beginnings. She had been to the town of Orla near the Polish city of Bielsk, where Chaim Kahan was born, and to Brest-Litovsk, where Chaim spent his early years after he married in 1864. She could describe the Brest-Litovsk house in detail. It had two stories, was built of stone, and had decorative brickwork around the doors and windows. It had once stood between the town post office and a government customs office. It was on a broad street that had an island in the middle that served as a taxi station.

From such a beginning, the story of the Kahans would flow smoothly, I was sure. Having read some of Verena's articles, I knew she was a fluent and expressive writer. She would arrange the events the Kahans' had lived through into a persuasive narrative—uncertainties would be confronted and analyzed, effects would be explained by their causes. It would be a compelling study of an important Jewish family.

Thinking about the book Verena would write made me consider my own. The stop-and-go style as I picked up the narrative with each visit to a new memorial, the gaps and loops in chronology—was this a proper way to organize history? But I was content that at least I had not imposed a logic that I had invented. I would deal in guesses, speculation, inferences. To my mind, nothing more was possible.

In Germany, when I mentioned that I was interested in Holocaust memorials, I was very often asked, "Did you see the *stolpersteine*?" They seemed to be everyone's favorite memorials, combining engineering ingenuity and aesthetic elegance.

A *stolperstein* (literally, stumbling stone) is a cobblestone-size concrete cube covered with a sheet of brass that has the relevant personal details stamped into it: name, year of birth, dates of deportation and death, if known. Most were installed in front of the individual's residence, but some were put at the place of employment.

A *stolperstein* lies almost flush with the pavement or sidewalk. Passersby are unlikely to actually stumble on it, but it catches the eye enough that they pause to read the inscription. In time, as the writing gets worn away, it sometimes becomes necessary to bend over to make out the words, and this can have the appearance of a reverential bow. The theory behind the *stolperstein* is, of course, that it takes very little to trigger memories of the Holocaust. That event is always at the edge of our consciousness, and the slightest tap brings it to life.

Stolpersteine were originally installed in Berlin before the practice spread to other cities. There are several in Hanover, in the street by the city center. I did stop when I came upon one. I did bend over to read the inscription. And I did for a minute consider the tragedy of this Hanover Jew whose life came to an end before it should have. The theory behind the *stolpersteine* certainly seemed correct. It didn't take much to get me thinking about the Holocaust.

As I continued on my walk, I came upon several more *stolpersteine*, and increasingly I grew annoyed. As much as the next man, in fact probably more than most, I believe it's important to remember what the Nazis did. But I prefer not to be nudged and prodded to do so. That's why I like memorials to be set off by fences or announced by signs or otherwise conspicuously marked. When the mood comes on me to see a Holocaust memorial, I know where to go.

My next stop was Vienna, and I looked forward to seeing how the Holocaust memorials there managed to take into account the zigzag maneuvers of Austria during World War II and after. How did the country manage to remember itself as the "first victim" of Nazi aggression, a designation Austria embraced after the war, even though it had been Hitler's enthusiastic partner almost as soon as he came to power?

There is a memorial in Morzinplatz in a small park near the

site of the old Gestapo headquarters that I had planned to see, but after reading about it in my guidebook and seeing a photo of it, I decided to skip it. Even at a distance it irritated me.

The photograph shows a bronze figure of a man surrounded by heavy boulders. The effect is of a doorway, and the man seems to be exiting from darkness into light. He wears a suit, a bit bedraggled but several cuts above the striped uniform of the camps. If not exactly jaunty, the man nevertheless does not look like someone who has endured great deprivation.

The memorial conveys a sense of looking forward. The horrors of the past seem to be set aside. The man looks out on a new world, in which he is ready to take his place. This perspective is confirmed by the inscription: "Here stood the House of the Gestapo. To those who believed in Austria, it was hell. To many it was the gates to death. It sank into ruins just like the 'Thousand Year Reich.' But Austria was resurrected and with her our dead, the immortal victims."

Five sentences, four implicit claims. There was an ideal Austria that stood apart from the evil done in its name. Those who believed in this ideal Austria, and not only Jews, suffered at the hands of the Nazis. The past is past, a new day has arrived, and all Austrians are united as they move into the future.

A few memorials that I had seen are designed to avoid any reference to a country's behavior during the Holocaust. Others incorporate an apology. And some are self-serving.

I headed for Albertinaplatz in the city center to have a look at Alfred Hrdlicka's Memorial Against War and Fascism. It stands directly behind the State Opera House and alongside a tourist information bureau, so that one can see a Mozart opera, plan an excursion, and contemplate the Holocaust memorial all in one afternoon. Tourists thronged the area, heading to various venues. It set up a chaos of concerns, with emotions of different valences bouncing off each other like electrons in a turbulent chemical reaction.

The memorial covers a small plaza of fifty square feet and comprises five elements, an arrangement that was needed to meet Hrdlicka's complex purpose. He meant to encompass a large swath of history. A paired set of large stones, one of which honors those who were killed in the Nazi death camps and the other of which honors all victims of the war, including fallen Wehrmacht soldiers, is set at one corner of the plaza. Another element is dedicated to the victims of an Allied bombing raid. Their bodies lie interred beneath the large stone at another corner of the plaza. There is also a thirty-foot-high granite piece with the imprint of an excerpt from Austria's 1945 Declaration of Independence that repudiates Germany's annexation of 1938.

The different varieties of victims, the conflation of events usually kept apart—that makes for more than enough ambiguity for any memorial to try to handle, but the fifth element of the memorial raises the stakes further. At first glance it appeared to be an indistinct block about three feet high, but close up the details became clear. I could make out the bearded face of an elderly man wearing a yarmulke and holding a brush. It was a representation of an old Jew scrubbing the streets.

Nazi cruelty often took the form of a theater of sadism. Not just cruelty but cruelty performed for public enjoyment. Jews forced to pick up snow off the street with a spoon, Jews having their beards cut off. In the Kielbasin camp outside Grodno, a Gestapo officer seized an elderly Jew and forced him to eat a pile of excrement in front of the assembled prisoners. The leader of Grodno's Judenrat was required to lead the march evacuating the ghetto wearing a clown hat and playing the fiddle while the Jews walking behind him sang "Yidl Mitn Fidl" (Yiddle with His Fiddle), the song from the hugely popular Yiddish movie of the same name—a demonic touch that turned Jewish culture lethally back upon itself.

Having Jews scrub the streets was a repeated episode in the Nazis' theater of sadism, so how could Hrdlicka's use of the same image not be troubling? But rather than back down, Hrdlicka argued that critics had too narrow a perspective. Yes, what the Nazis did was evil, but in his portrayal evil was transcended. Humiliation accepted was humiliation overcome. That sort of strategy is of course a staple of Christian iconography. Christ on the cross is a moment of celebration, not defeat, and Hrdlicka made that connection explicit in an interview. He said, "Jews should learn from Christ . . . Christ died the most humiliating death of all—and what did the smart Christians make of it? An iconography for half the world. And if Jews complain that I use an act of humiliation as a symbol, that's their problem."*

Over time, the memorial lost its novelty and the kneeling Jew became a piece of public furniture. Passersby weary from shopping, concertgoers celebrating their newly acquired tickets, tourists tired of queuing up at the information center, all used the statue as a bench. In 1990, to rectify the problem, the statue was wrapped with strands of barbed wire. This was an addition blissfully oblivious of symbolism. The barbed wire does the job of keeping people from sitting. But the suggestion of a crown of thorns, such a central piece of Christ's Passion, is startling.

Some memorials incite argument; they appear intentionally provocative. Hrdlicka's memorial was like that for me, and his suggestion that Jews mimic Christian humility was particularly irritating. It wouldn't be enough for me to tell everyone I met how

*Matti Bunzl. "On the Politics and Semantics of Austrian Memory."

badly misguided Hrdlicka's memorial is. I wanted to have Hrdlicka seated across from me at a table so I could tell him to his face how he had gotten it wrong.

"Listen, my friend," I would say, "you are totally off base. Invoking Christian humility as the standard for Jewish behavior during the Holocaust is insulting, suggesting that Judaism isn't able to provide its own modes of judgment. In fact, consider what one of my own relatives did when Nazism descended upon France. Your notion of Christian apotheosis through suffering utterly fails to explain his behavior."

This is the story I would have told Hrdlicka. Roger Cholenay was married to Sula, my aunt. When the Germans overran France, Roger was in the French army, stationed in the Free Zone. In 1940, as part of the armistice agreement, Vichy agreed to limit the size of the French army. One of the first steps was to strip Jewish soldiers of military status, which effectively deprived them of any civic protection. Many demobilized Jewish soldiers were immediately interned or sent to labor camps.

Luckily for Roger, post-armistice France was in chaos, since no one had foreseen such a quick surrender. Instead of reporting as ordered to a demobilization point, he made his way to Gabarret, a town south of Bordeaux. In civilian life Roger was a dentist, and a friend had told him that the local dentist had fled to England. Though Gabarret was in the Occupied Zone, that did not necessarily make it more dangerous. Given Vichy's zeal in helping the German masters, it may have been less dangerous.

Roger took over the office of the departed dentist and began to see patients. Very quickly he became part of the community. His practice grew, locals greeted him on the street. He felt comfortable, at home. One evening he was in his corner bistro when a propaganda speech came over the radio. It was the usual attack on Jews as vermin and enemies of civilization. Those present, some six or seven regulars, listened in a sort of befuddled silence, and this made Roger angry. People he thought of as good Frenchmen and Frenchwomen seemed ready to accept this venomous message. He could not let it pass.

Standing up, speaking for all to hear, he declared, "I am Jewish," and walked out of the bistro without waiting for a response.

It was a brave thing to do, but also foolhardy. Maybe some in the bistro agreed it was time to take a stand—if not in defense of Jews, always a touchy subject in France, at least against the Nazi domination of everyday French life. But many French stood ready to denounce a Jew in their midst. The record of French behavior under the occupation is still debated, but it was not a good idea to test the odds. As it happened, there was a collaborator sitting in that bistro.

A priest in town who had links with the Resistance lent Roger a bike, and he left Gabarret without packing his belongings. Some thirty miles out of town, a farmer who was active in the Resistance let Roger hide in his barn. Once when Germans came through on a routine search, Roger hid in a hole in the barn floor that had been covered with planks. A German soldier passed right over him. Once he took the train to Paris, risking the danger that the Gestapo might walk through his car, checking IDs. His father, who was in hiding, was old and ailing, and Roger felt it his duty to see him.

In a perfect world, after listening to me, Hrdlicka would have apologized for his misguided view of Jews as a people passively accepting Nazi domination. In a perfect world.

The thoroughfare around Vienna's Am Hof square was crowded—if motion were translated into sound, it would have been a deafening cacophony. I juggled my city map, trying to orient myself.

A quick dogleg to the left, then through a darkened arcade for fifty yards, and abruptly I was in a plaza of pastoral serenity. This was Judenplatz, and the memorial I was looking for. As it happens, the speed with which I reached my goal stands in symbolic contrast to the many debates, proposals, and counterproposals that had been necessary to bring the memorial into being.

There had been six years between the selection of an artist and the memorial's unveiling in 1990. Several groups had objected to the project—shopkeepers on Judenplatz who were afraid business would suffer, neonationalists who resented all things Jewish, cost-conscious citizens. The usual suspects. But also one surprising constituency: Vienna's Jewish community.

When construction on the memorial began, it revealed that the site overlay the remains of a synagogue dismantled in 1492, a time of ferocious anti-Semitism in Vienna. One hundred Jews were imprisoned in that synagogue and burned to death. Construction of the memorial would render invisible the traces of that crime.

Why, asked these critics, should the Holocaust be the event marking the saga of Viennese Jewry? Didn't that story go farther back than fifty years? Shouldn't Jews learn the full extent of their ability to survive? Ultimately, the remains of the synagogue were preserved in an underground museum that has an entrance at one end of the plaza, and that arrangement allowed the building of the memorial to proceed.

There is another noteworthy item in Judenplatz, placed some distance apart from the memorial. It is a statue of Gotthold Lessing, the eighteenth-century philosopher and playwright. The title character of his play *Nathan the Wise* is modeled on his friend the Jewish philosopher Moses Mendelssohn. The play argues that Jews could have noble souls, a controversial proposition for the times.

The statue has an aggressive quality. One foot is on a pedestal, so that the leg is bent at the knee and the body given a forward thrust. The head is cocked to one side. The arms are held away from the body, as if preparing for action. Maybe the aggressive pose is meant to show Lessing's strong response to critics of his play. But I saw another implication, one that justified placing the statue in proximity to a Holocaust memorial. Some 160 years after the controversy surrounding *Nathan the Wise*, many Austrians, falling in with the Nazi line, still treated the Jews as not fully human.

The Holocaust memorial, which dominates Judenplatz, was designed by Rachel Whiteread, a British sculptor of renown. Whiteread came to wide public attention when she won England's prestigious Turner Prize. Her *House* was a commentary on London working-class domesticity, which doesn't obviously suggest an artist capable of creating a Holocaust memorial. Whiteread has herself remarked that she doesn't consider memorials a natural fit, and she was surprised when she was offered the Viennese commission. In the event, some critics were put off by the austerity of what Whiteread created, but most were impressed.

What I saw was a sandstone-colored four-sided piece of reinforced concrete, twenty-three feet wide by thirty-three feet long by thirteen feet high with roughly textured surfaces. It seemed no more than an elegant box. Walking closer, I saw that its four sides were inscribed to suggest shelves with books, making me think of a library. The Jews as People of the Book? But that interpretation would leave out all the blacksmiths and butchers and beggars who ended up in the same gas chambers as Jewish lawyers and philosophers. Whiteread's library seemed to me to imply something more general—a world devoted to civilized discourse.

But it is a library with a most unusual feature. The books are stacked so that their spines point inward rather than outward. The effect is to indicate that the structure is hollow. There is an inside space where one presumably could read the titles and names of authors emblazoned on the book spines. But, tellingly, this space is unreachable. The double doors etched into the front of the memorial lack doorknobs, which is like getting an invitation to enter that is simultaneously canceled. Or, to put it more generally, we are invited to take note of the Western tradition of civilized discourse and also the Nazi plan to make it inaccessible. They wanted to take it out of circulation.

I circled the memorial, scrutinizing its features. The recurring vertical lines of the book edges were perpendicular to the horizontals of the shelves in a way that pleasingly emphasized the strict formality of the box. The sandstone color was just the right shade to underscore the artifice of the construction without being intrusive. There was a harmony to the overall composition. What I was looking at was, in fact, as much a sculpture as it was a memorial. Several memorials I had seen were erected by government committees or civic boards, and it was pointless to criticize them in terms that could apply to objects in a museum. The memorial on Judenplatz could stand up to that kind of criticism. It was beautiful.

Even as I came to that judgment, I knew that it was problematic. Should a Holocaust memorial, which honors those who died in mud and squalor, be beautiful? Lost in the pleasure of looking, completely absorbed by the memorial's elegance, wouldn't a viewer forget what the memorial stood for?

As I left Judenplatz, I glanced back at the memorial. An attractive young woman was posing for a friend to take her photograph. It wasn't going to be a typical tourist snapshot. She torqued her hips, presented her profile, generally deployed her body as a fashion model might. The memorial was a backdrop for a photograph that could appear in the pages of *Vogue*.

How often does life provide just the right event at just the right time? My doubts about the wisdom of making Holocaust memorials beautiful were reinforced. Beauty, I was being shown very clearly, is our culture's free-floating currency, and it can be used however, including frivolously.

Whiteread's memorial, with its depiction of a stylized library, offers an addendum to the usual Holocaust narrative. We are typically reminded of how the Nazis slaughtered Jews in the millions. The Nazis acted with impunity, certain that the Jews were weak and defenseless. But at the same time, the Nazis believed that Jews were powerful enough to contaminate all of the world's culture with their pernicious ideas. Books were carriers and they had to be quarantined.

Among the investments the Kahans made when they lived in Berlin was in the publishing firm Petropolis. Petropolis began in Saint Petersburg, moved to Berlin and then to Brussels and finally to New York. It published Russian-language works, mainly contemporary but also classics, and some of the writers were certain to have irritated Nazi sensibilities. Nikolai Berdiaev promoted a variety of existentialist Christianity at odds with Nazi dogma. Ilia Ehrenburg was a Jew and a Communist. Dostoevsky was not easy to categorize, and all the more dangerous for that reason. But it was the publication of Alexander Pushkin's collected works that would have been most irksome.

Pushkin's maternal great-grandfather was African, given as a gift to Peter the Great. Pushkin was proud of his African blood, boasting of it in his poetry. A serial seducer of women, Pushkin saw nothing wrong with homosexuality, treating it as cause for banter and not condemnation. A parody of the tsar earned him an exile from Saint Petersburg. That the Kahans supported publication of a writer who in his life and works treated the Nazis' bugaboos of sex and race and political authority so casually was gratifying to me. Of course, Petropolis's publication list was likely not noticed by the Nazis, and would have only slightly nicked their grandiose self-image if it had been. But on this trip, as I was time and again confronted with a picture of the Nazis' power, even small pinpricks of resistance were satisfying.

My next stop was Budapest, in another country that behaved badly during World War II. But while Austria is trying to forget its history, the present government of Hungary has decided to rewrite history. One blatant instance of that policy is the recently erected memorial in Budapest's Liberty Square. The memorial invokes the Holocaust, but it's hard to call it a Holocaust memorial. It's really a funhouse Holocaust memorial, where reality is reflected as a distorted image.

The figure of an angelic young man opens his arms to the sky in a gesture of innocence. In his right hand he holds a double cross, Hungary's national symbol. Swooping in on him from above is a monstrous eagle, its talons aimed squarely at the cross. As the accompanying text makes clear, the young man symbolizes Hungary, and the eagle is Nazi Germany. The memorial marks the German invasion of Hungary in March 1944. There was indeed a German invasion on that date, but Hungary, far from innocent, was from the beginning of the war a member of the Axis alliance. As the Red Army closed in and the war was clearly lost, Hungary attempted to sue for a separate peace. It was to forestall Hungary's surrender that Germany invaded.

As the memorial distorts those last days of the war, it also distorts Hungary's treatment of its Jews. The Holocaust that followed the German occupation was one of the most terrible in Europe, and it was largely the work of the homegrown Fascist movement Arrow Cross. Some 437,000 Hungarian Jews were sent to German-run killing facilities in Poland over the course of just fifty-seven days in the early summer of 1944.

When I was in Budapest, there were constant demonstrations against the Liberty Square memorial. A counter-memorial, in the form of short biographies of deported Jews and various forms of memorabilia, had been set up a short distance from the official statue. A police detail was on alert as a constant stream of tourists who had presumably come to look at the official memorial gave all their attention to the counter-memorial instead. The counter-memorial is makeshift where the official memorial is grand, its message is understated where the official memorial blares out the government line, but I wanted to believe that quiet subversion could carry the day.

When I was there, it was a bright, brisk afternoon. There were picnickers on the lawn behind the statue. Dogs running, kids playing, young women sunning themselves. But I told myself it was a picture of contingent pleasures. The uncertainties about Hungary's history could burst forth at any moment. Though in fact the dogs kept running, the kids kept playing, and the young women kept sunning themselves.

I looked forward to seeing the memorial honoring the Swedish diplomat Raoul Wallenberg. The one in Liberty Square had left a bad taste. Being reminded of Wallenberg's courage and his moral strength would serve as an antidote. Relying on his privileges as a Swedish diplomat, Wallenberg had saved thousands of Hungarians Jews by placing them in safe houses under his protection.

Directives from Stockholm ordered him to stop the practice, since it put Sweden's neutrality at risk, but Wallenberg persisted. He was a hero, and the Holocaust has need of heroes, especially in Hungary.

His memorial is in a small yard behind the Great Synagogue of Budapest on Dohány Street. After the Nazis occupied Hungary and Arrow Cross was given free rein to work its malice, the synagogue was transformed into a collection point for Jews en route to the killing camps. Thousands died from malnutrition and disease, and hundreds more were murdered at random. When Budapest was liberated by the Red Army, there were too many corpses to dispose of properly. They were buried in a mass grave in the synagogue courtyard.

I had to pass through this courtyard to get to the Raoul Wallenberg Memorial Park. The park is dominated by the *Tree of Life*, a sculpture in the shape of a large willow tree. The several hundred metallic leaves bear the names of Jews who died in the Holocaust. It was the gaudiest Holocaust memorial I had seen on my trip. It would not have been out of place in front of a Las Vegas hotel. But the crowd of visitors was enthusiastic and I began to think I was being an old grump, out of touch with current taste. Maybe selfies with the memorial as background, such as were being snapped all around me, were the twenty-first-century equivalent of laying a wreath.

Behind the *Tree of Life* was a more modest memorial, a plaque honoring those who stood up against Arrow Cross, including Wallenberg. But it seemed an afterthought to the *Tree of Life*, and in fact it got hardly any attention from tourists.

It was crowded in the park, hard to move about without getting in the way of someone's camera eye, and I saw no reason to stay. Any commemoration of bravery during the Holocaust is welcome, and Wallenberg was exceptionally brave. But he deserved something better than this carnival atmosphere.

A few hundred yards farther on in the neighborhood, at the edge of Budapest's former ghetto, there is another Holocaust memorial, as unvisited as the Wallenberg Memorial Park was overrun. And the setting, the dreary backyard of an apartment house complex, is more in tune with the dominant mood of the Holocaust. A figure—it could be either a man or a woman—lies prostrate on the ground, arm outstretched in hope. The hand points in the direction of a gold-plated figure atop a forty-foot treelike limb. A quote from the Talmud, "He who saves a single life, saves the world," refers to the Swiss diplomat Carl Lutz, who served in Budapest at the same time as Wallenberg and also saved many Jews. As a diplomat in Palestine in the 1920s, Lutz aided German settlers there, which gave him some standing in negotiating with Adolf Eichmann, the Nazi commandant in Budapest. Eichmann, who seems to have had a nasty sense of humor, referred to Lutz as "Moses."

Lutz devised the *Schutzpasse* (diplomatic protection letters), which Wallenberg adopted as a strategy to protect Budapest's Jews. Though the letters had no legal force, the Nazis accepted them as valid, perhaps because there were too few to be worth bothering about. But when the effectiveness of the letters became widely known, forgeries abounded. Eichmann, presumably savoring the cruel irony, put Lutz in charge of culling these forgeries, in effect making him executioner of those he was trying to save.

My guide for these two memorials was Madeline Warner, who had been recommended as someone who lived through the terror of 1944. Afterward we went to what she said was her favorite café in Budapest, and Madeline recalled her experiences from that time. This is what she told me:

When the Germans and Arrow Cross began their attack on Budapest's Jews, she was a girl of ten. She and her mother were arrested, and the two of them were herded toward the banks of the Danube along with eleven others. To save bullets, Arrow Cross often bound Jews into groups so that shooting one would cause all to fall into the Danube to drown. At the last moment, Madeline said, their would-be executioner noticed a larger group of Jews being herded down toward the river some hundred feet away, and he hurried over to take part in what would be a more spectacular murder.

Though I of course didn't say so, I found Madeline's story improbable. It didn't fit what I knew about Arrow Cross, whose goal was to kill as many Jews as possible, as quickly as possible, in whatever manner was near at hand. But I let her remarks pass without comment. Even if she hadn't been subjected to the mental torture of near murder, she had endured a horrific moment in Hungary's history. She was no less a Holocaust survivor than those who owed their lives to Wallenberg and Lutz.

Listening to Madeline reminded me that the Holocaust has left its mark on people who had very different wartime experiences. Those who survived the camps, obviously, but also those who were forever separated from their family by the wartime chaos, those who hid in forests, enduring extreme privation, those who lost every material possession, leaving them destitute. The list goes on.

Is there a calculus of suffering? Proximity to the cause is not a reliable indicator. Some camp survivors remain silent about their ordeal while their children, born after the war and living on safe shores, insist they suffer deep mental anguish. In some cases, indeed, it's not the children but the grandchildren who have claimed injury. Psychologists have a term for this syndrome— "inherited trauma." That refers to mental processes, but it may be easier to comprehend as a physical disease. Memories of the

Holocaust acting as a microbe, at times dormant, at times aggressive. The course of the disease defies explanation, and for those who suffer from it, that can be proof that the Holocaust itself defies logical explanation.

My mother's view about how the Holocaust affected her life has always struck me as admirable. It comes through in a taped interview made for Steven Spielberg's Shoah Foundation. The foundation collects remembrances from Holocaust survivors, and that is why my mother was included. But she begins the interview by declaring that she doesn't think of herself as a Holocaust survivor because she didn't suffer as others had. However, she fits the legal definition that was crafted once courts began considering claims for restitution for the pain and loss caused by the Nazis. A survivor was any Jew who lived for any period of time in a country that was ruled by Germany or its allies.

For my mother, the period of time was five months, ending with an escape to Portugal, and then on to the United States. That journey was harrowing, several times skirting disaster, but till then life under the occupation had been beguilingly calm.

When France surrendered in May 1940, my family was in Arcachon, a resort on the Atlantic. Responding to the interviewer's question, my mother says, "We were lying on the beach and lying next to us were German officers. They were"—she struggles for the right word—"they were *correct.*"

The interviewer interrupts. "Amazing. Sunbathing with the Gestapo."

"Wehrmacht," my mother says, insisting on not making her experience of the Nazi occupation appear worse than it was.

The interviewer asks about assimilating to American life, and my mother says, "In all my years in Europe, I never worked. When we came to America I had to work. My first job was in a chocolate factory. The smell made me nauseous. When I came home after work, the first thing I did was to put an orange to my nose to make me forget the chocolate."

My mother's life in Europe had not been a rich young woman's constant round of parties and outings, all frivolous pleasures. But neither was it controlled by a nine-to-five clock as it came to be in America. Though my mother surely regretted the change in circumstances, she did not consider it a catastrophe. She had, after all, escaped the Nazis. Indeed, though that nauseating smell of chocolate was a measure of how her life had diminished in America, it was also a declaration of how lucky she was compared to many others who had suffered much worse at the hands of the Nazis.

My mother's attitude regarding what happened during the war evolved into a policy. She refused ever to visit Germany. She never bought German products and didn't like speaking German, though she was fluent. She even had to be persuaded to watch a German movie. She hated Germany, but it was a hatred that was sharply defined. Sometimes my mother spoke about the Nazi barbarism that killed Alexandre and ten other members of his family, or about how Aronchik fell into despair after seeing his son and wife and mother-in-law arrested and sent to Auschwitz. And sometimes she spoke about the events that led her to that chocolate factory with its nauseating smell. But not consecutively, not as if they fit together in a single whole.

I respected my mother's hatred of Germany, but I couldn't match it. She knew the victims of the Nazis firsthand, and that intimate knowledge fueled her emotion. I learned the unhappy facts only later, and it was hard for me to sustain my anger. It came and went, depending on the circumstances.

One of the few arguments I had with my mother was when I

bought a Volkswagen, ignoring her boycott of all things German. My mother didn't have to stop to consider which German product to boycott, she boycotted them all. I didn't have that wholesale approach. I each time had to stop and calculate if a boycott was warranted, and sometimes I got it wrong.

A friendly auto mechanic told me a Rabbit was the best car for climbing the icy hills of the upstate New York town where I was living. Every time I made it up Ithaca's State Street without skidding, I felt justified in my purchase. But then spring would arrive and the ice would melt and any car would have served as well. By May of each year, I would be feeling guilty for not properly honoring the members of my family killed by the Germans.

There is a Holocaust memorial on the bank of the Danube at one of the spots where Jews were shot by Arrow Cross and their bodies thrown into the river. Some fifty pairs of cast-iron shoes are lined up, toes facing the river. They are of all kinds—worker boots and elegant oxfords and spike heels and children's slippers, and together they suggest a lively and diverse community cruelly destroyed. It was unlike any other memorial I had seen in its use of everyday elements, and I was taken by this ingenuity. But it also reminded me of a question that nagged at me even before I started my trip. Holocaust memorials seemed to come in so many different styles, with so many kinds of constituent elements, that the idea of a Holocaust memorial threatened to disappear into chaos. Is there any classification system that can account for the whole range of existing Holocaust memorials?

A friend to whom I had complained about the problem suggested I look at the work of the nineteenth-century American philosopher Charles Sanders Peirce. Peirce's writings are remarkably intricate even by the standards of academic philosophy, and

I don't pretend I can follow him very far. I wouldn't bring Peirce up if it weren't that some of his writings, at a superficial level to be sure, are germane to my difficulty. Though Peirce of course knew nothing about Holocaust memorials, he provides a way to think about them.

Peirce posits three main elements—symbol, icon, index. A *symbol* gets its meaning because society accepts the connection between the word and the thing. "Cat" refers to a cuddly four-legged creature because we agree to take it as such. There is no inherent reason for the connection. An abstract form—Berlin's Memorial to the Murdered Jews of Europe, for example—refers to the Holocaust because we agree to take it as such. There is no inherent connection between the memorial and what it represents, only a general agreement that one exists. An *icon*, by contrast, closely resembles what it represents. A stick figure in a graph stands in for a human being, a picture of a cigarette with a bar across it means No Smoking. Rapoport's Warsaw Monument to the Ghetto Heroes is an example of an icon. The men depicted in that memorial are identifiable as men who fought in the Ghetto Uprising. Peirce's last element, the *index*, is exemplified by the memorial on the bank of the Danube in Budapest.

An index, for Peirce, points to something that is not present but that is inherently connected. Paw tracks are an index that a bear has passed this way. A scent of perfume is an index of a woman who has left the room. The shoes by the Danube are an index of lives cut short by the Arrow Cross. Looking at those shoes, I was made aware of those who once enjoyed a life in Budapest. A construction worker who put in a hard day's work, perhaps, a business executive with a salary big enough to dress in style, a society woman who, by the look of the shoes, could have had a passion for dancing, along with a range of other Budapest citizens—all were here but now were gone, though I thought I could make out the thin vapor of what they once had been.

The Open Society Archives, part of Central European University in Budapest, is devoted to researching current international human rights violations, but it finds time to remind people of what happened in Hungary during World War II. Given the government's efforts to rewrite history, there's much work to be done. Nora Bertalan, the public programs coordinator, had a hand in carrying out the OSA Yellow-Star Houses project. We met in her office several months after the project had concluded, but Nora was still excited about what had been achieved.

She said, "It was illegal, so we had to organize everything secretly, using social media a lot, and then we did everything in the course of one night. It had to be done."

This was the context, as Nora explained it. In June 1944, Budapest's mayor decreed that all 220,000 Budapest Jews had to leave their homes. They were to relocate to selected apartments around the city, where they would be forced to live in extremely cramped conditions. Jews were allowed to leave these quarters only between 5:00 p.m. and 9:00 p.m., which meant shopping when many goods had already been bought. Subsequently, Jews were prohibited from leaving their residences at any hour. The Nazi edict was precise on one point. Each of these buildings had to "mark their street entrances with a yellow star, which must be kept permanently intact and clean." The sign had to be a six-pointed canary-yellow star measuring 30 centimeters in diameter on a 51-by-36-centimeter black background—another example of the Nazis' penchant for declaring cruelty in a bland bureaucratic style.

On the night of June 14, 2014, exactly seventy years after the Nazi edict was published, members of the OSA placed a Jewish star on eighteen hundred houses in Budapest that had once been used as "Jewish houses." A notice was also posted that suggested some public acts that could be performed in front of the house—reading the original law, group singing, conversing with neighbors about Budapest's behavior during World War II.

Nora said, "Some of the yellow stars were torn down, and there was some trouble when people gathered. There are groups who see nothing wrong with the original yellow stars. But I think that we succeeded in our plan. People began to think about our history."

In the larger scheme of things, with Jews killed in the millions, forced relocation might not appear so bad. But who makes those judgments? For those who endured it, that moment was traumatic. Getting kicked out of your home could appear the penultimate step before disaster.

Some years ago, when I was in Baku, I had a look at the Kahans' former apartment. It had several notable features, but two stood out for connoting the good life. In the dining room, there was a floor button that allowed the mistress of the house to alert the kitchen staff to send out the next course. That button implied a domestic life of comfort and prosperity. The view from the living room balcony gave out on a large stretch of the city as it sprawled toward the harbor. That view could make you believe you had climbed high on Baku's social ladder. It must certainly have been a very fine place to live, but there came a time when the Kahans were forced to leave.

When the Bolsheviks gained control of Baku in 1920, they immediately requisitioned space in private homes. The Kahan apartment on Nicolaevsky Street, soon to be renamed Lenin Boulevard, was judged luxurious enough to accommodate an important commissar. That he was the commissar in charge of the newly

nationalized oil industry was likely meant as a snub, a daily reminder to the family that their time had passed. Once mistress
here, my grandmother Zina now had to attend to the menial
needs of a new master—arranging his meals, making sure his
bed linen was routinely changed. The Kahans would not only
be uncomfortable on the streets now patrolled by the Reds, they
would also be made to feel out of step inside their own home.

It was like being mugged and then having to care for the
mugger, but Zina adjusted. Indeed, she seems to have charmed
Commissar Alexander Pavlovitch Serebrovsky. Some sort of flir-
tation arose, on his side anyway. I can imagine how that went—
Serebrovsky advancing his romantic cause with remarks about
pipeline capacity and barrels per year, hoping to win Zina's heart
with visions of the glorious workers' paradise that was around
the corner. That's just my fantasy, of course, I have no way of
knowing exactly what passed between them. But there was one
piece of hard evidence that the commissar was smitten. He provided Zina and her children with the permit, not easily available,
that allowed them to exit Azerbaijan. It should have been hard
leaving a home that had provided much pleasure, but by then
Baku had lost its luster, and Zina moved on without regret.

The Kahans' apartment on Schlüterstrasse in Berlin was also
much more than just a place to eat and sleep. Table talk at New
York dinners made the apartment appear as the fixed point
around which family life was organized, though to my preteen
imagination, it sounded more like a railroad terminal with
people of all sorts constantly coming and going. Shabbat services
were held in the *Berlin zimmer*, which could accommodate some
seventy worshippers. Besides the thirty family members who
lived in the immediate neighborhood, numerous friends and
acquaintances would show up, drawn by the presence of a Kahan
cousin who was a renowned cantor. For the High Holy Days,

rabbis from remote towns would come, so many that when they stayed overnight some had to sleep on the floor. The image of these sprawling rabbis evoked a place that was endlessly accommodating, constantly exciting.

When the *Berlin zimmer* was not used for Shabbat services, it became a salon. Linen tablecloths were laid out along with bone china cups and saucers, and a magnificent *plat de ménage*. Some prominent German Jews would show up. Walter Benjamin came for literary conversation, Zalman Shazar, a future president of Israel, discussed politics. The apartment provided the Kahans with much comfort and pleasure, but here too, when it was time to get going, the Kahans packed up and left.

The Kahans' apartment in Paris was on Rue Jean Carriès. There were two rooms in the attic that the family let stand empty. These extra rooms were a bet on a future when bourgeois comfort would give way to the high luxury the Kahans had enjoyed in Baku and Berlin. When the future turned down instead of up, the Kahans departed the apartment with no qualms. They had always known betting on the future was no sure thing.

A comparison with Aronchik and his family is telling. The Kahans lived in a series of apartments that provided comfort and pleasures. But their attachment to them was unsentimental because they assumed there was always something comparable at the next stop.

For Aronchik, the apartment on Square La Fontaine appeared to be the final destination. It was a symbol of the unexpectedly good life he had made for himself and his family in France. The street name was appropriate. It brought to mind the serene image of children tucked in their beds listening to parents reading those famous fables about a peaceable animal kingdom. In that kingdom, it was as if time had stopped. Everything would be exactly the same at the next reading and the reading after that.

Aronchik, having reached an optimum moment in his life, must have hoped that time would stop for him and his family also. I think that was why the new furniture he bought was so important to him—the weight of the sofa and table and armchairs was ballast to secure him and his family in place. As there had been nothing better before, he could imagine nothing better after.

Saarbrücken is a town in western Germany, near the French border. During World War II, it was the site of a Gestapo prison, which was an administrative unit outside the Final Solution apparatus. In practice, that was a distinction without a difference. Its location meant Saarbrücken could serve as a way station for trains from France carrying Jews and others the Nazis deemed "socially undesirable." Some were sent on to the camps in the East, some remained in Saarbrücken. But almost all were killed.

I had considered going to Saarbrücken to see the memorial there but then decided not to. The town didn't fit my itinerary, and, moreover, the memorial had been designed by Jochen Gerz, whose Hamburg memorial I had already visited. Like that one, the memorial in Saarbrücken is hidden underground. So what would I learn by going to the Saarbrücken memorial that I couldn't learn by reading about it?

Gerz's radical approach to memorials suggested an artist who didn't trust his art. He felt he had to hide what he had created. But Gerz had his reasons. Almost from the first moment people started to think about Holocaust memorials, they saw them as a special case. The sculptor Henry Moore, who was on the 1957 panel that rejected all three hundred proposals for a memorial at the Birkenau killing camp, put it this way: "A very great sculptor—a new Michelangelo or a new Rodin—might have conceivably achieved this. The odds against such a design turning up . . . were enormous."

Moore's point, that the unique horror of the Holocaust made representation of it uniquely difficult, is widely accepted. All the memorials I had seen tried to work through this problem in one way or another, with varying degrees of success. Gerz turned the problem into a blueprint. The Holocaust can't be represented by something the eye can see? Very well, how about something the eye can't see?

Gerz created his memorial clandestinely. Working at night, he and his team removed several dozen paving stones at a time from the square in front of Saarbrücken Castle, the seat of the Provincial Parliament. Each stone was then engraved with the name of one of the 2,146 Jewish cemeteries that existed in Germany before World War II. And then the stones were replaced facedown in the square.

The memorial accepts the impossibility of representing a monstrosity that exceeds human understanding. All that can be done is to imply the afterlife of what had been obliterated and desecrated. Though Germany's Jewish communities were no longer on this earth, the soul of Judaism endured. The inscriptions on the bottoms of the stones were a message from a vanished world.

Just to be sure that everyone got the message, Castle Square (Schlossplatz) was renamed Platz des Unsichtbaren Mahnmals, or Square of the Invisible Memorial. There was a street sign to that effect. Now people knew that they were not just walking but walking with purpose. They were honoring Jews killed in the Holocaust, whether they intended to or not.

Saarbrücken was basically like other memorials I had seen. It was a remembrance of the Holocaust. But it was different in one respect. It memorialized not people but places—cemeteries. Cemeteries are of course first of all places where bodies are buried, but because I was at that moment so concerned with the history of the Ripps and the Kahans, I thought about another function they serve. Cemeteries set family relationships into a final alignment.

Gita Ripp, my mother, is buried in New Jersey in a plot with her mother and sister. Monia Ripp, her husband and my father, is also buried there in what is essentially the Kahan family plot. Aronchik Ripp is buried in Paris's Pantin cemetery, alongside his father Lev and his sister Sula and her husband Roger, and also several of his in-laws. That is the Ripp family plot.

If there hadn't been a war, my father would certainly have been buried in the Pantin cemetery. My guess is that my mother, following her husband's lead, would have been buried there as well. She would have gone over from the Kahan camp to the Ripp camp. That's speculation, of course, and things might have played out differently. In fact, when the paths of the Kahans and the Ripps intersected in Paris in the 1930s, the relationship between the families was fluid, with allegiances still to be determined. In a sense my father and mother were trophies in a competition. One family would win what the other lost. I have more than a sideline interest in the outcome. It saved my life.

Monia worked as an accountant, putting his diploma from the Berlin business school to use. It was an okay job, nothing great. Leisure time was spent almost entirely with his family. The range of his activities was circumscribed. He stayed within the Ripp circle, just as my mother stayed within the Kahan circle, making the odds against their meeting pretty high.

Gita was in Paris and away from her family for the first time as the result of several abrupt decisions. She had dropped out of the Berlin gymnasium after finding she didn't like math as much as she thought she did. She then enrolled in art school but dropped out of that too. In Weimar Germany, art school meant more than learning how to draw and sculpt. As she put it, "Student life was pretty rowdy, not really suitable for a young girl from a good Jewish family." She came to Paris to learn interior decorating, a course of study that required neither math nor intense partying.

In Paris there was a wide network of friends, acquaintances, and business partners of the Kahans that Gita could rely on to provide a social life. Moses Eisenshtadt had served as the Saint Petersburg *Kazionnyi ravin* (official rabbi), part of the government's plan to create a modernized rabbinate. It was through his rabbinical duties that Eisenshtadt met Chaim Kahan. About a week after Gita arrived in Paris, Eisenshtadt invited her to dinner at his home.

Monia also had a connection with Eisenshtadt, though a more tenuous one. Eisenshtadt was originally from Nesvizh, where he had been acquainted with Monia's father, Lev Ripp. They were friends but not close friends. Friendship, in any case, was not the reason Monia was invited for dinner. The Eisenshtadts hoped that a meeting between Monia and their marriageable-age daughter might spark into romance.

I can picture the evening, my mother having described the key moments. Dinner passed with polite conversation, guests and hosts just getting acquainted. The emotional temperature was set on low. After dinner, Monia convinced the group to go to Café Prada on Avenue de la Grande Armée. The band there played Russian songs, which my father, ever nostalgic for his early life in Grodno, couldn't resist. The party broke up around nine o'clock, with goodbyes said on the sidewalk outside the café. In a gesture that caught everyone by surprise, Monia offered to escort my mother home. This was a deliberate romantic choice—he chose my mother instead of the Eisenshtadts' daughter.

That evening did not lead directly to marriage. A social barrier stood between the Kahans and the Ripps. A few weeks later, my mother and father ran into each other outside Galeries Lafayette. My mother found the encounter a pleasant surprise. But my father, as he told my mother later, found it embarrassing. One of his shoes was visibly torn, and he was sure she would take that as a sign of all that divided them.

Indeed, after Gita and Monia married and when the Kahan family and the Ripp family occasionally met, though the mood was amiable, a sense of economic and social disparities was never far from the surface. At one point, Zina lent Aronchik money to meet a business debt. It was a friendly transaction, but there was no ignoring the fact that one person was the lender and the other person the borrower. The marriage was a joining of two families with different ways of being in the world. Gita and Monia had to choose—necessarily one of the families would be more prominent in the newlyweds' life.

At first it seemed that my mother would move into the Ripp sphere. She and Monia spent most of their leisure time with Aronchik and his wife and Sula and her husband. They all lived in the same neighborhood, they picnicked together, went to the movies. Often they took their meals together. Aronchik's stencil business was beginning to do well, and Monia thought about joining him.

But ultimately Monia was drawn into the Kahan sphere. He was wary, sensing that the Kahans' habit of mixing business duties and personal allegiances would leave no room for his own ambitions. But with his marriage came the necessity of financial stability to start a family. He wanted to leave his accountant job, and Aronchik's stencil business, though promising, was still in its uncertain beginning stage. He couldn't resist my granduncle Aron's offer.

Aron had met a man who ran a cafeteria-style restaurant in

Germany and was looking for an investor to establish a similar place in France. Never one to do things by halves, Aron bought a house on Boulevard Haussmann that was large enough to seat two hundred patrons. There was an on-site bakery to provide bread and desserts. A laundry attended to the dining linens and staff uniforms. Aron gave the cafeteria a name redolent of foreign-style efficiency—Kwik. My father took on the job of manager.

There were problems from the start. The waiters were incompetent and devious, pocketing money meant for the till. The cashier often didn't show up, requiring my mother to step in. More critically, the partner vanished, leaving my father to do the daily food shopping in the market. Adding that early morning chore to the day-to-day managing of the restaurant was stressful, especially as my father had no training or aptitude for that work.

My mother put it succinctly: "He didn't know the difference between a carrot and a potato." This was my mother looking back, when she could find humor in the situation. But at the time, when the success of Kwik hung in the balance, my father's efforts were not laughable. He threw himself into the job, substituting energy for knowledge.

The boundary between work and domesticity was blurred, as was usual with the Kahans. Gita and Monia now lived with my grandmother Zina and granduncle Aron in the apartment on Rue Jean Carriès. The apartment had a maid's room and another for the live-in seamstress and the two in the attic that the family still wasn't sure what to do with. The apartment was big, but I'm sure my father found it cramped. It was a long way from that moment when he drove his brother and sister around Paris in a convertible and life seemed full of possibility. But my father accepted his narrower horizons. Providing for his family came first.

How blurred was the line between work and domesticity?

One anecdote is telling. My father had the habit of exercising before he set off for the market at five in the morning. It was a way to ease into the rigors of the day, and he held to the practice with strict regularity. One night my mother felt she was about to give birth to my older brother, and she awoke my father in the middle of the night to drive to the hospital. Jumping out of bed, still half asleep, my father stumbled into the next room and began his exercise routine. The anecdote became part of my family's lore, and though it has a humorous aspect, it also shows how deeply committed my father was to making Kwik a success.

Despite his best efforts, Kwik failed, as anyone with knowledge of the leisurely eating habits of the French could have predicted. He had bet on the notion that financial stability was most important, putting down his dreams as collateral, and he had lost. But, unexpectedly, he got something better than financial stability. That is, indeed, the ultimate point of this story. If my father had rejected Aron's offer and gone into the stencil business with his brother as he had been tempted to do, we would have stayed in France. We would have been caught up in the Final Solution. As it was, my father, my mother, my brother, and I followed the Kahans to the safety of America.

The last stop on my journey was Paris, and almost immediately after my arrival I went to see the Shoah Memorial in the Marais, the old Jewish Quarter. The day was warm and sunny, and the many tourists swarming through the fashionable neighborhood came armed with ice cream cones in one hand and iPhones in the other. I was apprehensive that there would be a carnival mood in the museum as there had been at other Holocaust sites. But inside there was a reverent hush, though it was crowded.

Visitors milled around near the entrance, where a huge cistern-like form symbolized the chimney of the killing camp ovens. I made my way to the outside patio, where there were fewer people.

Three stone walls, each some twenty feet high and forty feet long, were inscribed with the names of Jews deported from France. What was novel here was that the names were arranged according to the year of departure on a train to the camps. Alexandre Ripp was grouped with others in the 1942 category. The Final Solution is one long dismal story, but I found it worthwhile to be reminded in what chapter Alexandre figured. From the start of this trip I had been concerned to understand why I and my family had escaped while Alexandre and most of his family had been trapped and murdered. This memorial showed me that the best answer might simply be a repetition of the question in slightly altered form. We escaped because we left France in 1940. Finally, all speculation about right and wrong choices aside, the best that could be said was that it was all in the timing.

In the winter of 1939, my father, mother, older brother, and I left Paris and drove to the town of Mont-Dore, near Vichy. Though there was no panicked mass exodus such as followed the German invasion a year later, the war in Poland made many Parisians fear that the city was next on the list of bombing targets. But there was another reason for the trip besides a flight to safety. My mother was a strong believer in the benefits of mountain air for young children, and Mont-Dore lay near the Massif Central. My father took the train to Paris to work during the week and returned to Mont-Dore on the weekends.

In the spring of 1940, we moved to Arcachon, a resort near Bordeaux. When my mother later described that trip, she joked that it was to balance the mountain air of Mont-Dore with some sea air. But no one was joking back then. We were in Arcachon on May 10 when the Germans invaded France and still there on June 17 when France surrendered. The Germans did not immediately institute anti-Jewish policies, but anyone who paid attention to what was happening in Germany and in Poland could have made an educated guess as to what was in store.

The best chance to escape the gathering danger was through Spain to Portugal and then to points beyond, usually the United States or South America. The road was geographically direct but bureaucratically tortuous, in most cases requiring four documents—a transit permit to cross Spain, a visa for entry to Portugal, a U.S. visa, and, just to start down that road, an exit permit to leave France. That document was available only from the German occupying forces, and was given only to those who could show a Portuguese visa, and not necessarily to all of them. The Germans were in conqueror mode, and their treatment of the defeated population was often arbitrary.

Lolia, my mother's brother, had been living in Lisbon for several years, supervising the remaining outpost of the Kahans' oil business but also spending a lot of time in high society. That proved to be one case when dancing at balls and dining out at elegant restaurants produced a worthwhile result. Thanks to an acquaintance he had struck up with a Portuguese diplomat, Lolia was able to secure a Portuguese visa and Spanish transit permit for my family.

The times were hectic, communications faulty, crossed signals routine. A bureaucrat in Lisbon sent the visas to the Portuguese consulate in Bayonne instead of to Bordeaux, the city nearest Arcachon. Portuguese visas typically had short expiration dates, in a futile attempt to impose order on the mass movements of people trying to escape disaster. By the time my parents figured out that the visa was in Bayonne, it had expired.

Deciding to chance it without a visa, my parents drove to Biarritz and applied for an exit permit from the German administration there. My mother described the office they were ushered into as very large, with a Mussolini-style desk at one end and an angry German officer seated behind it. When my parents displayed their Polish passports, he started shouting that such a country no longer existed, that it was now a colony of the Third Reich, and that, besides, my parents were dirty Jews.

Looking back at my family's efforts to get out of France, I am struck by how many decisions were involved, how often my parents had to weigh the risks, always with little understanding of the odds. Upon our return to Paris, there was a letter from the Portuguese consulate in Bayonne saying a new visa had been issued and could be picked up when convenient. Maybe presenting the letter to the German authorities in Paris would suffice to get an exit permit. Or maybe such a step would bring unwanted attention. The encounter with the German officer in Biarritz had made my parents, nervous to begin with, highly anxious.

The Kommandatur, the Paris headquarters of the occupying German forces, was in the Hotel Majestic on Avenue Kléber. Upon inquiring, my parents were told that maybe they were entitled to an exit permit, maybe not. The request would have to be reviewed. My parents should come in to the Kommandatur and bring all relevant documents with them. There had been stories of people entering the Majestic and never being heard from again. But finally my parents decided to risk it.

No matter how many times my mother told the story, she always paused over one detail. The Majestic had a long staircase leading to the administrative offices on the mezzanine. It was marble, so each step she took resounded like a harbinger of doom. In her mind, Nazis had taken on the form of monsters, unpredictable and death dealing. But, remarkably, a permit was provided with little trouble. This was October 4. The indicated deadline for leaving France was October 7.

So long after the fact, it's hard to know with any certainty why my parents got that exit permit. It's possible that remnants of the earlier policy of forcing Jews out of German-occupied Europe still lingered. On the other hand, on October 3, the French police, under pressure from the Germans, had summoned all Jews in Paris to register with the local gendarmerie as a prelude to large-scale arrests and detentions. What is certain is that after saying goodbye to family and friends and storing all our furniture, we left Paris on October 6, 1940.

To be filed under "Department of Small Satisfactions": After the war, my parents learned that almost immediately after our departure from Paris, several German officers requisitioned our old apartment for living quarters. They were bitterly disappointed that the furniture had been removed, cursing the concierge for permitting that. I can picture it, the Third Reich's finest warriors stamping their feet and shouting because they didn't have the sofa they expected to have. It's an image to treasure, something salvaged from the ruins of a way of life.

After briefly stopping in Bayonne to pick up our visas at the Portuguese consulate, we reached the French border town of Hendaye. There we had to disembark because Spanish trains ran on tracks with a different gauge. We walked across a bridge to the Spanish town of Irun with all our belongings piled on a cart, topped by my tricycle—my mother's wistful hope, as I see it now, that we were on the road to tranquillity. However, once in Spain, my father was immediately arrested by the pro-Fascist Spanish police because his passport was Polish. Poland had been overrun by the Germans but its government had technically not surrendered, and that made my father a "captured combatant."

Fortunately, my father had just two months prior turned forty.

That put him over the draft age, and hence he was not a "captured combatant" after all. After an anxious twenty-four hours, he was released from prison, and we boarded the next train to Lisbon.

Two weeks later, Hitler met with Franco at the same Hendaye railroad station that we had passed through. Negotiations produced no agreement on the terms for Spain to enter the war on the Axis side. But the meeting was proof of a common perspective, and the Spanish border police would thereafter surely have been less likely to let Jewish refugees pass through their country without very careful scrutiny. I doubt that my father's age-related excuse for not being classified as an enemy combatant would have been accepted.

At the conclusion of *Casablanca*, the Ingrid Bergman and Paul Henreid characters escape to Lisbon. The film portrays Lisbon as the opposite of Casablanca, as a city of freedom and peace. But in real life, escaping to Lisbon would have landed someone in a city that was very like the Casablanca portrayed in the movie. It was the home base for thousands of refugees eager to move on but caught in a bureaucratic logjam. There was a thriving black market for the exit documents required for the last leg of the journey to safety, many of which turned out to be forged. Spies from both the Axis and Allied sides kept tabs on the bustling café life, where plans deriving from varying degrees of patriotism and self-concern were hatched.

Portugal was officially neutral, but as a dictator Prime Minister António Salazar was inclined to look favorably at fascism, and he accommodated Germany in various ways. A prominent German Jewish writer was kidnapped by Nazi agents from a café in broad daylight. Some Jews were arrested by the Gestapo while on incoming trains. And in October 1940, the pro-Fascist Secret

Police were put in charge of issuing entry visas, reducing the number considerably.

But as a devout Christian, Salazar was repelled by Nazi racial practices, and this attitude filtered down to the bureaucracy. Some Portuguese consulates, particularly in Bordeaux and Budapest, continued to issue visas to Jews even though that contradicted stated policy. Those with the right connections, such as we had through my uncle Lolia, could still find a way. Once in Portugal, Jews found that rules governing refugees were often laxly enforced. My mother had an acquaintance who would appear as required at a police station when her visa expired. "This is the last time," the bureaucrat would say as he extended her visa another thirty days, just as he had numerous times previously.

But Salazar's sympathy for the Jews extended only so far. He believed they were carriers of radical "cosmopolitan" ideas that could infect a Portugal that had largely stayed apart from European politics. To guard against that possibility, most Jews who arrived in Portugal were settled in "fixed residences" in the suburbs and countryside and not allowed to travel outside the locality without the permission of the Secret Police.

For these Jews it was a meager and bleak existence. But we had an apartment in Lisbon, and there were even occasional trips to Estoril, the beach resort two hours' drive from the city. Also, while most of the refugees depended on the Red Cross, the Quakers, or international Jewish charities for support, we were able to make our own way, thanks to Lolia and the vestiges of the Kahan business interests in Portugal.

Yet we were very much like all the other Jewish refugees in Portugal in our desperate efforts to obtain a U.S. visa. Twice a week my parents would travel up the coast to Oporto. There was a rumor that the U.S. consulate there had a more flexible policy regarding passports than the embassy in Lisbon, where the rules were adhered to with maddening precision. The U.S. quota system was calculated on data from 1890. Two percent of a foreign-born group's population at that time could be admitted. This favored the British and Irish, who had little need of a safe haven—their allotment of 84,000 spaces out of a total of 164,000 went mostly unused. In our favor was that most Poles were trapped in Poland by the German occupation, so though the Polish quota was small, there were few applicants.

Nevertheless, it took five months to get our visas. A sponsor in the United States had to guarantee that new arrivals would not draw on public assistance, and the sponsor himself had to be vetted to show financial stability. Tax returns, bank statements, affidavits of other assets, even police records had to be submitted for inspection. Aron and Zina had made it to America a few months earlier, but such a short residence disqualified them as sponsors. Finally, a cousin of Zina's agreed to sponsor us, thus underscoring the fact that though our passports said Ripp, key parts of our escape to America were made under Kahan auspices.

As a final piece of good fortune, we were able to secure places on the *Serpa Pinto*, one of the very few passenger ships still making the transatlantic journey. After a brief stop in Bermuda, where customs officials searched everyone's luggage in the hope of confiscating an illegal shipment of diamonds that was rumored to be on board, we docked in Hoboken on March 16, 1941.

My six-year-old brother had already started school in Europe, but his education had always been oddly out of sync with the surroundings. In Paris, he had been sent to a Russian-speaking school, which would have been suitable if we lived in Grodno. In Lisbon, he had gone to a French lycée even though we had just left Paris. In America, in contrast, he was enrolled in Bentley, a small private school on the Upper West Side where the instruction was in the English he was fast acquiring.

Every day after school, my brother went with his granduncle Aron to the corner drugstore on Eighty-sixth and Columbus. In those pre–Duane Reade days, drugstores had soda fountains, and my brother—in what I now think of as a decisive step toward becoming American—always ordered a chocolate malted, a drink never even imagined anywhere in Europe. Indeed, for all of my family, America was where our lives at last fell into step with our surroundings.

The site on Avenue Kléber where the Hotel Majestic once stood is now occupied by the upscale Peninsula Hotel. The promo sheet notes that in its previous life as the Hotel Majestic it was the site of the famous meeting between Marcel Proust and James Joyce. The promo sheet didn't mention it, but anyone familiar with the history of twentieth-century literature has heard the story. The meeting didn't go well. Proust arrived late, Joyce was drunk, and neither admitted reading the other's work. But the meeting nevertheless marks an important occasion, and the hotel has a right to boast. The promo also notes that George Gershwin wrote part of *An American in Paris* when this was the Hotel Majestic, and that it was where Henry Kissinger signed the Vietnam peace agreement. A brief sentence mentions that the Kommandatur occupied the building during World War II.

When I went to have a look, I found that the opulence smothered all signs of the past. Certainly, what I was most interested in, vestiges of my parents' desperate attempt to get exit permits, was nowhere to be found. The offices occupied by the German staff had been redesigned as a guest-welcoming area. That marble staircase, with the steps that rang their doomsday sounds, was gone. What was needed, I decided, was a memorial, preferably something hard to miss right in the middle of the lobby. It was

the only way I would have been able to find my connection to
the past.

By the time my journey had brought me to Paris, I had been to
five countries and seen thirty-one memorials, and each time I
wondered how well a memorial gave me an understanding of
my cousin Alexandre's ordeal. Paris had numerous Holocaust
memorials that I could have seen, but I had a new idea. Why not
skip the memorials that intervened between my cousin's experience and my attempt to understand it? Paris was the starting
point on my cousin's road to Auschwitz, and several stops on that
tragic itinerary were also within easy reach. Like a pilgrim walking the Via Dolorosa, I would understand Alexandre's suffering by
going to where it had been inflicted. I didn't expect a religious
experience, but it would be a pilgrimage.

Alexandre was arrested with his grandmother, and with seven
thousand other Jews who had been rounded up in the July 1942
police action, they were taken to the Vélodrome d'Hiver, a
stadium that was used for biking competitions and boxing
matches. Parisians usually referred to the velodrome with the
nickname Vel' d'Hiv, signaling its status as a familiar part of
the city. But till then no one had thought of it as a place of pain
and deprivation.

Accounts by those who lived through the Vel' d'Hiv impris-
onment describe excruciating conditions. The heat, already
summertime oppressive, was made worse because all the windows were nailed shut to block escape. The shifting crowd raised
clouds of dust. There were only twelve toilets, all of them soon
blocked and unusable. People relieved themselves in stairwells

and against the walls. Supplies of food and water were soon exhausted. There were no doctors. No medicine was available. Three people died from heart attacks. Ten women committed suicide by jumping from the upper sections, one of them carrying a baby in her arms. Contact with the outside world was blocked, causing great anxiety among the families that had been separated. Many men, including Alexandre's father, had managed to avoid arrest because they had been warned of the roundup. Some women, including Alexandre's mother, had been arrested separately and sent directly to the prison camp in Drancy.

One feature in the descriptions of the velodrome especially caught my eye. The glass ceiling had been painted green to work as camouflage during air raids, and this bathed the whole interior in an aquamarine light. I couldn't be sure if Alexandre had seen any of the suicides or if he had noticed people relieving themselves against the walls. I couldn't know what his gaze had taken in. But anywhere he looked would have had a ghostly tint that would have made him believe he was in a frightening new world.

A fire destroyed part of the velodrome in 1959, and the rest was demolished to make room for a row of apartment houses. The Bir-Hakeim Métro stop is the one closest to where the velodrome once stood, and there is a plaque there commemorating the 1942 roundup. Across the street from the station there was a more elaborate memorial, also with a plaque. On the day I was there, flowers had been placed at the site. A short walk farther on toward the Seine, on a plaza largely hidden by large plants along its perimeter, there is a memorial with seven figures, including two children, in postures of uncertainty and exhaustion. Though the accompanying text does not mention the Vel' d'Hiv, the reference is clear. The platform that the figures sit on is sloped to invoke the bicycle track of the velodrome.

Three commemorations of the Vel' d'Hiv within walking distance of one another. To me, the redundancy only underscored the absence of what once was here. I would not be able to follow Alexandre's footsteps as I had planned. And, most regrettably, I would not be able to grasp how it felt to look, as Alexandre had, at a world painted over in a green tint that made everything appear ghostly and strange. The glass ceiling was gone, demolished along with the rest of the velodrome.

After four days in the Vel' d'Hiv, Alexandre and his grandmother were transported to Beaune-la-Rolande, a camp an hour south of Paris. The camp can stand as an indicator of France's fortune during the war. It was built in 1939 to house British and Canadian expeditionary forces, but they didn't stay long enough to need long-term housing. The camp was then designated to hold German POWs, but there were none. In 1940, the Germans interned French POWs there before sending them on to Germany.

When Alexandre and his grandmother arrived, they found living conditions better than in the Vel' d'Hiv. There were working toilets and the barracks had double-tiered bunks to sleep on. There was an infirmary. Photographs show prisoners strolling in the area between the barracks, some in shirtsleeves to better take advantage of the summer sun. One man sits at a makeshift desk, writing a letter. But nothing ameliorated the deprivations. Food was in short supply. There was hardly any medicine, and four children died as a result. Prisoners were crammed into ramshackle barracks. The camp was ringed with barbed wire and overlooked by guard towers. There was no pretense that this was anything but a prison camp. However, the defining fact about Beaune-la-Rolande was not physical but bureaucratic. It was designated as a transit camp, a stopover in an itinerary that ended in Auschwitz.

When plans for the deportation from the camp were first formulated, Prime Minister Pierre Laval of the puppet Vichy government proposed including children under twelve. He did not want Vichy to be burdened with the care of orphans, oblivious to the role that Vichy had in turning the children into orphans. The Germans ignored Laval's suggestion, concerned that deporting children would provoke a public that to this point had been largely docile.

That decision gave Alexandre a temporary reprieve from a death sentence but also condemned him to constant anxiety. He would have to make his way without his grandmother's help. On the eve of her departure from Beaune-la-Rolande, she sent a letter to the concierge of the house where Alexandre lived—she couldn't write to his father directly without revealing his hiding place. The letter was eventually passed along to my father after the war.

"Dear Mme. Bourdier, I am with Alex at Beaune-la-Rolande camp, but tomorrow I must leave and my grandson will remain alone. He is sick, he is hungry. He cries all day and night. I beg you to come immediately and look for my grandson, bringing for him two warm garments, two shirts and something to eat. If you know the address of a Catholic family who can take him in, please let me know. Perhaps that can be arranged."

The remarks about Alexandre's suffering brought me closer to understanding what he experienced—but not all the way. It was his grandmother's voice I heard. And the plan to save Alexandre was of course something only an adult could have conceived. What Alexandre thought about his predicament remained a mystery.

I had read David Drake's authoritative history of the German occupation, in which he has this to say about Beaune-la-Rolande: "French gendarmes beat hysterical mothers (some of whom were still lactating) with their rifle butts in order to separate them from their screaming children and toddlers. At the end of July and the beginning of August, five rail convoys of adult deportees and children over twelve left Pithiviers and Beaune-la-Rolande and went directly to Auschwitz. The little ones remained behind."*

This wasn't much help to me. The more Drake tries to capture the general horror of the situation by including vivid details, the less his account has to do with Alexandre—his mother was not lactating, she was not even there. Drake notes that the children appeared skeletal. Probably that's how Alexandre looked, but "probably" was not good enough for me. I wanted the indisputable facts of Alexandre's ordeal. Hannah Arendt, reporting on the Eichmann trial, calls the Beaune-la-Rolande action "one of the most horrible of the many hair-raising stories told in Jerusalem."† What Arendt heard was indeed a story, and putting the tumultuous events into a coherent narrative necessarily meant paying little attention to any single case.

After the war, the camp was demolished, but I hoped some traces remained. I learned that the Musée-Mémorial des Enfants du Vel' d'Hiv in Orléans held the records for the Beaune-la-Rolande camp, and I e-mailed a query to the archives department. The reply informed me that after the war the camp barracks had been put up for auction. Most were bought by local farmers, but one ended up in the town of Ladon, where it was used to store paint. Remarkably, that barracks, number four, was the one to which Alexandre had been assigned, and the museum had acquired it. Grateful for my good luck, I made ready to travel to

*David Drake. *Paris at War, 1939–1944*, 268.

†Hannah Arendt. *Eichmann in Jerusalem: A Report on the Banality of Evil*, 164.

Beaune-la-Rolande, to put myself in the place where Alexandre had endured hunger and extreme discomfort.

But a subsequent e-mail exchange with the Orléans museum brought bad news. Only one-tenth of the barracks remained intact, which considerably dimmed the aura of authenticity that I was pursuing. But that was not the worst of it. After the museum had tracked down barracks number four, it was put on display in Orléans. As a curatorial strategy, that made sense. In Beaune-la-Rolande, an agricultural school now occupies the site where the camp once stood, leaving no space for reminders of how Jews lived and died under the German occupation. In Orléans, the barracks would get public attention. But I had no intention of going to Orléans. Orléans had not been a stop on Alexandre's itinerary.

There was, however, one more site to investigate.

On July 7, 1942, Adolf Eichmann, who was in overall charge of deportations, had ordered that children under twelve be included in the convoys traveling to Auschwitz. Eichmann's order seems to have been ignored by German authorities in France, who did not want to spark any public outcry. But at the end of July, Eichmann's order was reinstated, and on August 28, Alexandre was transported to the holding camp at Drancy.

Drancy lies some seven miles outside of Paris, and I took the regional train that departed from Châtelet. I stupidly assumed that once in Drancy, I'd have no trouble finding signs of the old camp. Wasn't that Drancy's only claim to fame? Instead, I exited into a hodgepodge of small stores and dreary cafés that left me at a loss. The ticket clerk had to consult with a colleague before answering my query about which bus to take to the memorial. And then, a few minutes into the ride, I realized I had not asked at which stop I should get off. The driver was no help—that Drancy was once a prison camp for Jews was news to him. He suggested I ask some passengers, but I got only blank looks in response. It wasn't really surprising. Drancy is a *banlieue*, one of those communities at the periphery of Paris with a population largely of politically alienated and economically deprived Muslims. Their lives are consumed by daily hardships and complaints. There isn't much time left over to think about a memorial to something that happened so many decades ago. Given the anti-Semitism that prevails in the *banlieues*, a Holocaust memorial would attract even less interest. I got off the bus at random and stepped into a sudden rain shower. I had imagined coming to Drancy as a pilgrimage, a solemn ritual where every step signified a meaning, but it wasn't working out that way.

A ten-minute walk finally brought me to the site of the defunct camp. Across the street there was a museum, and I decided to have a look. The exhibits on the second floor spelled out the history of the Drancy camp. The complex of buildings was originally designed as public housing. When it was built, in the 1930s, both its design and construction methods were innovative. The freestanding buildings of five stories each had a repetitive design that was influenced by Le Corbusier. The U shape formed by the three buildings created a courtyard that could be used for different forms of recreation. A guiding principle was to set the buildings apart from the tumult of the surrounding neighborhood, a gesture toward tranquillity that the buildings' ultimate use turned into a cruel irony.

Construction on the project was halted when financial backing collapsed during the global depression. The Jewish prisoners who arrived in Drancy in 1942 were confronted with chaos. There were no rooms, only large hall-like areas where groups of seventy or more inmates were jammed together. They slept on straw mats. No electricity, no water, very few toilets, so that piss and shit collected in the stairwells. There was one feature that was suitable for Drancy's new use as a stopover on the way to Auschwitz: The five-story height of the buildings proved suitable for suicide, and there were several.

On my way out of the museum, I stopped at the information desk and asked if there was any documentation regarding Alexandre's stay in Drancy. I didn't expect much since what was there to learn at an information desk except maybe how many days a three-year-old boy waited before being put on a train to a death camp. I was surprised when after a brief computer search the attendant handed me a printout of Alexandre's Drancy ID card—ANF/9/5747—with the notation that he had been interned "avec Mme. Olga Liebermann."

This contradicted the historical accounts that asserted that the separation of children and relatives at Beaune-la-Rolande was permanent, as well as survivor memoirs that claimed that the children who were in Drancy had arrived and were housed separately from adults. And of course there was the letter Alexandre's grandmother had written on the day before she was scheduled to be deported from Beaune-la-Rolande. Against all this evidence, there was only the notation on Alexandre's ID card, and yet I was ready to accept that as persuasive. I wanted to believe that Alexandre's ordeal had been eased.

But, of course, even if I was right about his grandmother's presence, that didn't tell me what I most wanted to know. With or without his grandmother, Alexandre was still a three-year-old boy waiting to be put on a train to a death camp. I wanted to grasp how he had felt about what was happening to him, how he experienced his last days, and nothing in the museum's computer could help me with that.

I left the museum and crossed the street to the courtyard

formed by the three large buildings. At its open end were three memorials—a boxcar, a plaque, and a twenty-foot-high sandstone statue covered with Jewish religious symbols. An inscription on the base, from the first chapter of Lamentations, seemed to imply that just as insufficient piety among Jews had resulted in the destruction of the first Temple in Jerusalem, so the Jews bore some responsibility for the Holocaust. Normally I would have stopped to consider how the memorial illustrated this bleak idea, but at that moment I was not interested in memorials. They only pointed to the real thing. I was more interested in the courtyard in which the memorials stood. Alexandre would have walked in this very place.

There's a photograph of the Drancy holding camp that shows the courtyard as a place of surprising repose. No guards to be seen. Men and women, still in their civilian coats and hats, seem to be out for a stroll. One woman wears high heels. Boys in shorts and kneesocks look as if they are about to have a race. One Drancy inmate who survived the war recalled how on an early morning stroll in the courtyard he crossed paths with the camp commandant Alois Brunner, who after the war would be charged with crimes against humanity. The two men exchanged greetings as if they had met on a country lane before each went his own way.

But it was unlikely that Alexandre saw the courtyard as a place of leisurely pleasures. This was where buses were loaded up each morning to take Jews to the Le Bourget railroad station and from there by train to Auschwitz. Jews who resisted boarding were kept moving by the blows of the gendarmes, and even if Alexandre couldn't understand the reasons for the melee, he would have been infected by the anxiety and desperation circulating in the courtyard.

Several survivor memoirs note that among the inmates the future was often referred to as "pitchiboi"—a nonsense word, but it allowed conversations to go forward without the need to stop and speculate about what lay in store. "Pitchiboi" apparently was coined by some of the younger prisoners, who used it to refer to the moment when they would be reunited with their parents. Alexandre may have used the word, or at least heard it spoken.

I felt I was as close to understanding what Alexandre had experienced as I was likely to get. I could measure with my eye the dimensions of the courtyard where he walked. I had a sense of the anxiety that prevailed and that must have infected him. When he heard someone say "pitchiboi," he would have missed his parents desperately.

I believed I could grasp the psychology of his three-year-old mind, thanks to one other fact that I had learned from survivor memoirs. Upon arrival, the prisoners were issued ID numbers that they had to recite on demand. Children too young to memorize their IDs had them written on a cardboard placard that hung around their necks on a string. Alexandre was certainly adorned in that manner. His body was transformed into an advertisement for himself. Because what was written on a cardboard placard was fully sufficient for the world to understand him, he must have lost all sense of who he was aside from a set of numbers. His inner life, his identity—call it his soul—was hollowed out.

I had set out to grasp the very details of Alexandre's ordeal, that was the pilgrimage that had brought me to Drancy, but now that I had acquired that knowledge I wasn't sure I wanted it. I pictured Alexandre wandering robotically through a desolate landscape, a free-floating anxiety clouding his days. The image was so appalling that it was painful to keep in mind.

The Association pour la Mémoire des Enfants Juifs Déportés sounded like a source for more facts about Alexandre's mistreatment at the hands of the Nazis. I had enough of those and almost canceled the appointment I had made with Isabelle Sananes, who heads the association's branch in the Sixteenth Arrondissement, Alexandre's old neighborhood. But I was glad I didn't. Isabelle was far from the officious bureaucrat I expected. We met in Café Dix, on Place de la République. Isabelle's husband Pascal was there to translate as needed, but she did more than well enough on her own, her passion for her subject taking up the slack whenever her English faltered.

Her father was seventeen years old when he had been arrested for distributing leaflets encouraging Parisians not to cooperate with the German occupation. He spent the war in a labor camp, and returned home deeply marked by his contact with Nazism. At first he didn't want to talk about his experience. It was only after a while that he felt something had to be done to confront a public seemingly oblivious to what happened during the occupation. In particular, he wanted to remind France how children had suffered. They constituted a special category of victims. He decided to put up plaques in their honor in the schools they were attending when they were deported. That would show most vividly how young lives had been interrupted.

Isabelle had carried her father's idea forward, and I congratulated her on her good work, but added that unfortunately it was irrelevant to my purposes. Alexandre was too young to have attended school. He was a subcategory within a special category, and so his name would not be on any of the plaques that Isabelle's organization had installed in the schools in the Sixteenth Arrondissement.

Isabelle nodded, as if she had anticipated my remark. "We knew when we were putting up the plaques in the schools that there were children who were in exceptional circumstances. So we did something to honor them also. I think you will be satisfied with what we did," she said, and gave me directions to get where I should go.

From the Rue de la Pompe Métro station it was a short walk to Square Lamartine. A sign indicated it was named for Alphonse de Lamartine. I resorted to the tool of the quasi-educated, and Google provided Lamartine's CV. During France's Second Republic, he was an advocate for the abolishment of both slavery and the death penalty. He was a poet good enough to be elected to the Académie Française and to be awarded the Legion of Honor. There was more, and I began to think that any memory of Alexandre would be crowded out by the spirit of this famous *poète et homme politique français*. But once I entered the park that dominated the small square, I forgot all about Lamartine.

The park is the length of half a city block and some sixty feet wide, with trees running along both sides. There is enough space for a small jungle gym and a slide and for tricycles to maneuver. At the far end there is a water fountain drawing on an artesian well. Six-story buildings with flower-bedecked balconies overlook the park, adding to the serenity of the setting.

It took me a few minutes to find the memorial Isabelle had told me to look for. It was off to the side and discreetly placed amid some large plants. The main purpose of the park is for children to play in. The memorial has to fit itself in.

The glass tablet is some four by six feet and with an etching of two childish hands—stubby fingers, puffy palms—reaching for each other. There is an inscription: *Nombre d'entre eux vivaient à Paris dans le 16e arrt., parmi eux, 15 "tout-petits" n'ont pas eu le temps de fréquenter l'école. Passant, lis leur noms, ta mémoiré est leur unique sépulture.* (Numbered among those who lived in Paris in the Sixteenth Arrondissement, there were fifteen so young that they had not reached an age when they would have attended school.

As you pass by, read their names, your memory is their only grave.)

Fifteen names were etched into the glass: Daniele Baur, Tony Lambert, Berthe Lando, Juliana Rajcyn, Daniel Stepanski, and nine others besides Alexandre's. Yesterday those names meant nothing to me. Now they represented Alexandre's coterie. Like him they had lived in this neighborhood, played in this yard, eagerly waited for the day when they would receive their school uniforms. The memorial defined Alexandre's life in a way that made it more than its sad ending at the hands of the Nazis.

For a few minutes I stood and watched the children at play. All of them were between four and six or so, and I thought how sad it was that Alexandre's life had been cut short before he had played as these children were playing. But of course that was the wrong way to look at it. The point was that but for the Nazis, he would have been here now watching these children and recalling his own childhood games.

What would that scene have been like, a man looking back at a younger version of himself? I had trouble picturing how age looks at youth, and so I glanced around at the other people in the park to see if there was someone I could use as a model on which to build an image. There was a young couple embracing. Several nannies minding their young charges. One middle-aged man, a middle-level-manager type, was reading the newspaper. And I realized that the person in the park who could best serve as a stand-in for Alexandre was me.

SELECTED BIBLIOGRAPHY

James E. Young's *The Texture of Memory* (Yale University Press, 1993) and *At Memory's Edge* (Yale University Press, 2000) deserve special mention. The two books pointed me toward several memorials I otherwise might have overlooked.

The site www.memorialmuseums.org has an exhaustive list of memorials in Europe that I consulted.

The books and articles listed below were particularly useful, providing both facts and analysis.

GENERAL

Bathrick, David, editor. *Visualizing the Holocaust*, Camden House, 2008.
Epstein, Helen. *Children of the Holocaust*, Putnam, 1979.
Friedlander, Saul, editor. *Probing the Limits of Representation*, Harvard University Press, 1992.
Linenthal, Edward T. *Preserving Memory: The Struggle to Create America's Holocaust Museum*, Viking, 1995.
Ziebinska-Witek, Anna. "The Representation of Death in Exhibitions: The Case of the State Museum at Majdanek." *Ethics, Art and Representations of the Holocaust*, edited by Simone Gigliotti, Jacob Golomb, and Caroline Steinberg Gould, Lexington Books, 2014, 267–81.

AUSTRIA

Bunzl, Matti. "On the Politics and Semantics of Austrian Memory." *History and Memory*, vol. 7, no. 2, Fall–Winter 1995, 7–40.
Pauley, Bruce F. "Austria." *The World Reacts to the Holocaust*, edited by David S. Wyman, Johns Hopkins University Press, 1996.

AZERBAIJAN

Gefter, M. Ia, editor. *Monopolisticheskii kapital v neftianoi promishlennosti Rossii (1883–1914)*, Akademiia Nauk SSR, 1961.

Marvin, Charles. *The Region of the Eternal Fire*, W. H. Allen, 1888.

Pushkin, A. S. "Puteshestvie v Arzrum." *Polnoe Sobranie Sochinenii*, vol. 5, Khudozhestvennia literatura, 1975.

Suny, Ronald Grigor. *The Baku Commune, 1917–1918*, Princeton University Press, 1972.

Tolf, Robert W. *The Russian Rockefellers: The Saga of the Nobel Family and the Russian Oil Industry*, Hoover Institute Press, Stanford University, 1976.

BELARUS

Cohen, Morris Raphael. *A Dreamer's Journey*, Beacon Press, 1949.

Franklin, Jonathan. "Assimilation and the Jews in Nineteenth-Century Europe." *Assimilation and Community*, edited by Jonathan Frankel and Steven J. Zipperstein, Cambridge University Press, 1992, 1–37.

Howe, Irving. *World of Our Fathers*, Simon and Schuster, 1976.

Lederhendler, Eli. *The Road to Modern Jewish Politics*, Oxford University Press, 1989.

Lost Jewish Worlds, www.grodnoonline.org/lost_worlds/section_4_test.html.

Nathans, Benjamin. *Beyond the Pale: The Jewish Encounter with Late Imperial Russia*, University of California Press, 2002.

Rajner, Mirjam. "Chagall's Fiddler." *Ars Judaica*, vol. 1, 2005, 117–32, www.academia.edu/854036/_Chagall_s_Fiddler_.

Sobolevskaia, O. S., and V. S. Goncharov. *Evrei Grodnenshchiny. Zhizn' do katastrofy*, Nordpress, 1955.

Zandman, Felix. *Never the Last Journey*, Schocken Books, 1995.

Zborowski, Mark, and Elizabeth Herzog. *Life Is with People: The Culture of the Shtetl*, Schocken Books, 1962.

Zipperstein, Steven J. "Transforming the Heder: Maskilic Politics in Imperial Russia." *Jewish History*, edited by Ada Rapoport-Albert and Steven J. Zipperstein, Peter Halban, 1988, 87–110.

FRANCE

Arendt, Hannah. *Eichmann in Jerusalem: A Report on the Banality of Evil*, Penguin, 1963.

Drake, David. *Paris at War, 1939–1944*, Belknap, 2015.

Marrus, Michael R., and Robert O. Paxton. *Vichy France and the Jews*, Basic Books, 1981.

Nord, Phillip. *France 1940: Defending the Republic*, Yale University Press, 2015.

Pryce-Jones, David. *Paris in the Third Reich*, Holt, 1981.

Rosbottom, Ronald C. *When Paris Went Dark*, Little, Brown, 2014.

Weinberg, David H. *A Community on Trial*, University of Chicago Press, 1977.

Wellers, Georges. *De Drancy à Auschwitz*, Éditions du Centre, 1946.

Zuccotti, Susan. *The Holocaust, the French, and the Jews*, Basic Books, 1993.

GERMANY

Gerz, Jochen. Conversation about liberty and art. www.youtube.com/watch?v=QC3RtXir2IM.

Hoheisel, Horst, and Andreas Knitz. "Berlin Torlos—The Brandenburg Gate Is an Empty Place [Berlin 2003]." www.knitz.net/index.php?option=com_content&task=view&id=18&Itemid=32&lang=en.

LeWitt, Sol. "Paragraphs on Conceptual Art." *Artforum*, vol. 5, no. 10, June 1967.

Pinsker, Shachar. "Spaces of Hebrew and Yiddish Modernism: The Urban Cafés of Berlin." *Transit und Transformation*, edited by Verena Dohrn and Gertrud Pinkhan, Wallstein Verlag, 2010.

Polyan, Alexandra. "Productive Help in Russian-Jewish Berlin: The Union of Russian Jews in Germany." *Transit und Transformation*, edited by Verena Dohrn and Gertrud Pinkhan, Wallstein Verlag, 2010.

Williams, Robert C. *Culture in Exile: Russian Emigres in Germany 1881–1941*, Cornell University Press, 1972.

HUNGARY

Braham, Randolph L., editor. *The Nazis' Last Victims: The Holocaust in Hungary*, Wayne State University Press, 1998.

Yellow-Star Houses. www.yellowstarhouses.org.

POLAND

Arens, Moshe. "The Jewish Military Organization (ŻZW) in the Warsaw Ghetto." *Holocaust and Genocide Studies*, vol. 19, no. 2, 2005, 201–25.

Murawska-Muthesius, Katarzyna. "Oscar Hansen and the Auschwitz 'Countermemorial,' 1958–59." *ArtMargins Online*, May 21, 2002. www.artmargins .com/index.php/articles/311-oskar-1.

Snyder, Timothy. *Bloodlands: Europe Between Hitler and Stalin*, Basic Books, 2010.

Steinlauf, Michael C. *Bondage to the Dead: Poland and the Memory of the Holocaust*, Syracuse University Press, 1997.

Stier, Oren Baruch. "Different Trains: Holocaust Artifacts and the Ideologies of Remembrance." *Holocaust and Genocide Studies*, vol. 19, no. 1, 2005, 81–106.

ACKNOWLEDGMENTS

In writing this book, I was helped by many people in many places in many different ways.

Tatiana Kasataia made my visit to Grodno highly rewarding, providing me with archival material I never could have found on my own and also taking the time to show me around the city. In Hanover, Verena and Henning Dohrn were gracious hosts. Verena, who is writing a book about the Kahan family to be published in Germany in 2018, generously shared information her research had uncovered. I spent a memorable afternoon in a Paris café with Isabelle Sananes of the Association pour la Mémoire des Enfants Juifs Déportés, hearing of her work. In Budapest, Nora Bertalan took time off from her duties with Open Society Archives to explain the place of the Holocaust in today's Hungary. I enjoyed my friendly disputes with Ewa Junczyk Ziomecka about the history of Polish-Jewish relations, though neither of us convinced the other. Agata Tuszynska's affection for Warsaw was infectious and made my stay there a pleasure.

I am grateful to Eva Gossman, Michael Levine, Ylana Miller, Marty Miller, Howie Rosen, and Mirriam Rosen, all of whom offered encouragement and suggested changes that improved the manuscript. Three readers deserve particular mention for their close attention to the text, which saved me from numerous blunders and stylistic infelicities: Eleanor Ripp, Eric Lubell, and my daughter Alex Ripp (whose name is an intended echo of my cousin Alexandre's).

My editor at Farrar, Straus and Giroux, Ileene Smith, guided me with efficiency and expertise through the stages of the publishing process. Her super-capable assistant, Maya Binyam, responded patiently to my many queries. I thank Scott Auerbach, Cynthia Merman, and the rest of the FSG copyediting department for their meticulous work. Abby Kagan deserves credit for the book's design. Jeff Ward of JWDesign produced the map.

Charlie Read took time out from his other occupations to shoot the author photo. He also tutored me on book design.

Special thanks to my wonderful agent Melanie Jackson, who saw something worthwhile in an early version of the manuscript when there wasn't much there to be seen.

This is a book about family, and several family members were indispensable in its writing. My brother Paul Ripp, who lived through some of the events described in the book, was an invaluable source of information. Luckily, he has a better memory than I do. My parents Gita and Solomon Ripp and my grandmother Zina Kahan and granduncle Aron Kahan are deceased, but the book could not have been written without their recollections, some recorded and others I heard around the dinner table. They provided facts, but more important they described the anxieties and hopes and disappointments surrounding the facts.

My wife Nancy Kanach was a wonderful reader and editor. But her greater contribution was to dispense joy and good cheer that eased the occasionally wearying task of writing, and this at a time when she had her own demanding job to attend to. She has my huge thanks to go with my love.

Printed in the USA
CPSIA information can be obtained
at www.ICGtesting.com
LVHW091143150724
785511LV00005B/500